FALLS MEMORIES

GERRY ADAMS

FALLS MEMORIES

A BELFAST LIFE

ROBERTS RINEHART PUBLISHERS

Copyright © 1982, 1983, 1993, 1994 by Gerry Adams
International Standard Book Number 1-879373-96-3
Library of Congress Catalog Card Number 94-66263
Published by Roberts Rinehart Publishers
Post Office Box 666, Niwot, Colorado 80544

First Published in Ireland by Brandon Book Publishers Ltd.
Dingle, Co. Kerry

Drawings and map © Michael McKernon 1981, 1982

Cover painting of Massarene Street and St. Peter's
by Proinsias Ó Coigligh

Cover design by Steven Hope

Distributed in the United States and Canada by
Publishers Group West

For Colette and Gearóid

CONTENTS

Foreword   ix
The Lower Wack   1
In the Beginnings   7
Tuath na bhFál   19
The Union and the Unions   27
The Linen Slaves of Belfast   33
Saints or Sinners?   41
Falls Road Factionalism   49
Schools and Scholars   56
Dèja Vu   61
The Thirties and the Forties   69
My Aunt Jane   76
Bunking In   91
Snake Belts and Dog Fights   97
Wakes and Witches   102
Prods and Micks   108
Cocker and Company   119
Pawn Shops and Politics   128
Postscript   136
Notes   140
Select Bibliography   143

Foreword to the new edition

More than ten years have passed since *Falls Memories* was first published, and many of the places I wrote about then have disappeared. I was conscious of their passing on an individual basis, as one by one old familiar landmarks vanished in clouds of developers' dust, but the cumulative totality and finality of these demolitions comes as a shock as I glance through these pages and take stock of what was once our part of the Falls Road.

Now, from Dunville Street down, the road remains in name only and at the other end, Divis Street is even worse. A new, characterless, anonymous, windswept, wide-open expanse of tarmac, bisected and undermined by motorway, has replaced a colourful and busy thoroughfare of shops and pubs and people. The railings and RUC-machine-gunned and bullet-pocked walls of St Comgall's School remain. That's about it. The rest is gone, or going.

Above Albert Street the planners never even attempted to replace what they destroyed. There was talk of a dual carriageway and so, until recently, the front of the road, from Leeson Street down, was undeveloped and is only now after years of robust representations being *improved*.

The Clonard picture house has gone and the Christian Brothers' House. Gilliland's shop is now a bookie's and Patsy Ferris's greengrocery is an advice centre. But this part of the road isn't *too* bad. The Sports Bar remains and McPeake's, McCallion's and Harden's. Local GAA clubs have taken over Walsh's Bar and the bank but Daly's is the only pub left between Clonard Street and Castle Street and there are no public houses at all in the newly built back streets.

The nuns retain a presence on the front of the road and down the road St Peter's Pro-Cathedral has been elevated to a Cathedral, but St Finian's School stands empty and vandalised while St Vincent's is rejuvenated as a busy community project. A new St Peter's School for girls and boys, modern and long overdue, has replaced them. It sits in a new Falls of good houses, built in long main streets fringed by the cul-de-sacs dictated by counter-insurgency architecture. No more traditional street patterns with lines of terraced houses and scores of ways in and out. Now the Lower Wack has a few, more easily monitored main exits and entrances. Population control is the name of this particular game but the Falls is not so easily overcome.

Divis Flats have gone also, except for the infamous Divis Tower with its top storeys of British troops and their high-rise, sky-high view of us all. It remains by decree of the British Ministry of Defence, and in spite of popular feeling. The rest of the Divis slum went after over twenty years of campaigning by local people. For me this victory is one of the highlights of this period. Along with the successes of numerous community projects and the resurgence of the Irish language, the "Demolish Divis" campaign is a testament to the resilience of the people of the Falls.

However much the streetscape has altered, at times for the better and at times not, that resilience remains today. The local geography may have changed. The people have not. Part of a political statelet from which it is excluded, the Falls remains a place apart, a state of mind and even, at times, a political statement. But more than all this the Falls is its people.

This is as evident today as it was in my childhood and before. The courage, self-reliance, hospitality, generosity and good humour of the people of this part of Belfast is as strong now as ever it was.

These qualities are not confined to the Falls area, of course, and to claim a monopoly of them would be too parochial, even for Belfast people. These are universal traits but even this is hardly surprising. After all, aren't there Falls Road people everywhere!

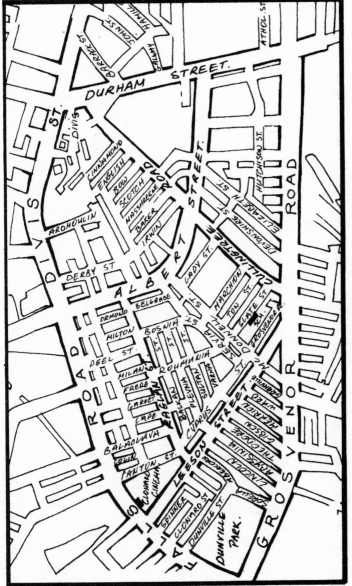

The Pound Loney and adjacent areas.

The Lower Wack

For since the civil modern world began
What's Irish history? Walks the child a man?
William Allingham

EARLY one bright Monday morning, I dandered along Sorella Street in the direction of the Falls Road. I hadn't been along this way in a good while but now, on impulse, I decided to venture into the area, curious to see how much the district had changed at the hands of planners. So instead of heading up Dunville Street, I strolled towards Abercorn Street North.

Here I used to live, spending an uneventful childhood playing rally-oh, kick-the-tin, handball and football, sprinkled with occasional forays against the Getty Street lads who were foolhardy enough to venture into our territory. It appeared to me at the time that our gang had a fearsome reputation, though I suppose that by today's standards we weren't really at all fearsome.

'I must be getting old', I said to your man.

'And sentimental', he retorted. 'You'll be saying next

that the weather was always warmer, the food more wholesome and the football better.'

'And so it was. Well, I mean to say, we had less distractions in those days. Look at the park, not a sinner in it. I remember when the place would have been black with people.'

'At ten o'clock on a Monday morning! The kids are at school', your man interrupted me scornfully as I gazed forlornly across a deserted Dunville Park.

'I suppose you're right', I admitted as I passed the wee gate of the park. Maybe I am getting old, I mused. I recalled older people telling me the same thing about their childhoods; and thought that such recollections must be coloured, not by any generation's monopoly on good weather and all that goes with it, but more likely by one's increasing and self-inflicted inability to participate in simple pleasures associated with childhood.

'No use getting philosophical at this hour of the morning', I muttered aloud.

'There's wiser locked up', your man suggested, leaving me to my own devices at the corner. I walked by Getty Street entry and then, stunned, I stopped and stared as I entered a new world — a waste land. On my left, behind hoardings, new houses were rising while on my right — emptiness. Gone was the rag store and Patsy's corner shop. All the old neighbours' houses had vanished, leaving a view, obstructed only by an occasional remnant of the past, right down to the Long Bar; while across from me in the distance stood the twin spires of St Peter's where Divis Flats raised their tower blocks to the heavens.

I stopped outside where Begleys had lived. Just an empty space. No wee girls swinging on the lamp-post now. Not even a lamp-post; just a broken pavement. But what of the neighbours? Scattered far and wide, no doubt; some dead, the younger ones married and living up the road, with a few lucky enough to win a house back in the old area, thus escaping the transport costs that a regular visit to the 'broo' demands. In a short while the district will have vanished, and those returning from exile in America or Long Kesh may well wonder at the changes as they pass through what is now a strange, alien landscape.

I passed Harbinson's corner and memories came flooding back. Of Sundays spent tickling trout in Kansas Glen, only to have our catch devoured by a great-uncle in Gibson

The Long Bar, Leeson Street

Street whose greatness was measured not least by his relish for fresh trout. Of double-decker candy apples with coconut on top. Of being slapped on my first day at St Finian's. Of pig's feet and matinées in Clonard picture house. Hopping the carts in Leeson Street. The 'reg' men and the wee man selling coal brick. The happy horse man and the refuse man.

Ghost stories told at gable ends and re-enacted on bedroom walls with nightmarish results. Over towards Raglan Street we played handball and heard occasional stories of Pig Meneely or Paddy-Me-Arse, two peelers well known to older people in the area. Or the Drango Kid, our nickname for their contemporary, an R.U.C. motorcyclist who scattered softball games of football or rounders with his forays down Balaclava Street into our part of the district.

Whispers about 'the boys' or an occasional witness to meetings of pale-faced earnest young men who, we gathered disinterestedly, had just 'got out'. Being chased by 'the wackey' while fleeing gleefully after hours from Dunville Park or after disturbing old men playing marleys at the shelter. Later still, but with less glee, being pursued by R.U.C. riot squads and, later again, by the British Army.

The rubble-filled waste land filled with ghosts as I headed along Ross Street. Years ago it had echoed to the clatter of millworkers crowding the pavement as they linked their way to and from work.

> You'll easy know a doffer
> As she comes into town
> With her long yellow hair
> And her ringlets hanging down
> With her rubber tied before her
> And her picker in her hand
> You'll easy know a doffer
> For she'll always get her man.

I headed across Albert Street and towards the Loney. Or at least towards where the Loney used to be. A few years ago when asked where you lived it was always 'down the Falls' as distinct from the area from Springfield Road upwards which, although on the Falls Road, isn't really 'the Falls'. It's 'up the road'. You see, we were from 'down the road', a clearly defined territory wedged between the Grosvenor, the Falls and Durham Street. Part of our district was called Leeson Street, a term which covered the streets from Leeson Street itself to the Grosvenor.

The Loney would have to have had flexible boundaries to accommodate all those who claim the status of former residence. The extent of its territory is thus often much disputed. Bingo Campbell, for example, swears that it was the streets bounded by Divis Street, Albert Street and Durham Street, though others, myself included, disagree.

In the early 'seventies the entire area became known as 'the Lower Wack', a local jibe at the British Army spokesmen's habit of talking grandiosely about 'the Lower Falls'. That is, when they weren't talking about some place on the other side of town known to everybody else as Ardoyne but which they persisted in calling 'the Ardoyne'. Later the Lower Wack became known in contemporary republican jargon as 'the Dogs', after the local I.R.A.'s famous 'D' company which a local wit christened 'D for Dog' during a period when their tenacity brought the area repeatedly to the headlines.

Since then, of course, the Falls has become a household name, and television coverage of riots, curfews and pogroms has made its small streets known to many who never had the privilege of experiencing them, their back entries, yard walls and the hospitality of their people.

Now, only that hospitality, and the people's resistance, remain; and as I stopped at St Peter's and reflected on the passing of a community, a wee woman approached me.

'You'd better watch yourself, son, there's Brits down at the Flats.'

'Thanks, missus', I replied as, startled out of my musings and brought back to reality by her warning, I retraced my steps and hurried, more carefully now, towards the crowded and relatively safer Falls Road.

My short walk had filled my head with memories. Stories of I.R.A. volunteers like Charlie Hughes, Paddy Maguire and Squire Maguire or Jimmy Quigley. I passed Alma Street and looked down to where Garnett Street used to be. Remember the day that Mundo O'Rawe was shot there? Remember hearing about the girl volunteer, her face streaming with tears and her body wracked with sobs as she tried to exact vengeance on a hovering helicopter with an aged .303 rifle which was too big for her to shoulder properly? I never found out who she was. Maybe she never existed. Just another story? You never know. I heard it said she stood there, on her own, firing away and all the time muttering 'You bastards, you bastards' to an implacable sky and a whitewashed wall, which had probably seen it all before. You see, they shot Mundo after he had been arrested. But then, I suppose that's the way it goes.

And what about local characters like Bunny Rice and Paddy-with-the-glass-eye? We had some crack with Paddy, God forgive us; but to tell the truth I was a wee bit scared of him. Remember getting called for supper: the long-drawn-out chant of 'Gerry, you're awanted for your dinner'. But life goes on. Still, it's strange to see gardens facing the Baths, though maybe there were gardens there in the first place. As I passed by McLarnon's shop I wondered what it was all like years and years ago.

'Somebody should write a book about what it was like here', I said to your man. 'Right from the very beginnings. Maybe I'll do it, if I get a chance.'

'Well, you'd better do it quick or nobody'll know where you're talking about', said your man back to me. 'It'll be like all the things you say you're going to do. The district will be completely gone and you'll still be spoofing about doing something about it. You'd wonder you never catch yourself on.'

'Oh yeah', said I. 'Well, we'll see about that. . . .'

In the Beginnings

This jewel that houses our hopes and our fears
Was knocked up from the swamp in the last hun-
dred years
But the last shall be first and the first shall be last
May the Lord in His mercy be kind to Belfast.

Maurice James Craig

THE early history of this part of Ireland is largely unrecorded and sources are extremely limited but despite this there remains some physical evidence that the Belfast area and the counties of Antrim and Down were inhabited by early man and woman, for many centuries BC.

In many parts of Ireland neolithic graves, dating from 3700 to 2000 BC, such as the fascinating New Grange in County Meath, serve as markers to the ingenuity and skill of this early civilisation. So also in the greater Belfast area there are two such reminders, both dolmens, one at Dundonald and the other at Ballylesson. The latter, which consists of a 'giant's ring' of stones around an even older tomb, forms a huge amphitheatre most likely used for some ceremonial or ritual purpose. The 'giant's ring' seems to date from about 1800 BC when the use of metal was first introduced to Ireland and the size of the enclosure shows that there must have been a substantial population in the area in the late neolithic or early Bronze Age times. These Bronze Age people also built a number of smaller tombs, enclosed in stone cairns on the summits of County Antrim hills and one example of these can be seen today, near the city, at Squires Hill.

About 500 BC with the coming of the Iron Age and a new wave of invaders the Celtic civilisation of Ireland, with its heroic sagas, began. This was the time of Tara, of Cuchulainn and of the Táin. In Belfast during this era McArt's Fort was built at the summit of Cave Hill. This was a promontory fort, approachable only from one side and it dominated the entire surrounding area. Today its site continues to dominate the city of Belfast and it was perhaps for this reason or perhaps because of its historical importance that Wolfe Tone and Henry Joy McCracken chose this spot, in 1795, to swear themselves to the struggle for Irish independence.

The Iron Age settlers also built the raths or circular fortified homesteads which are fairly numerous in the Belfast area. The Four Masters record the building of such raths during this period and the great fort at Rathmore near Antrim had a written history from the second century AD when it was known as the *Rath Mór Muigh Line.* It is to this period that George Benn in his *History of the Town of Belfast* (1832) dates the first mention of the 'parish of Belfast' when it is said to lie in the southern part of Dal Riada, an ancient division of the county of Antrim.

A village of *Béal Feirste* is believed to have existed at a fordable spot on the river Lagan which marked a boundary between the counties of Antrim and Down. This village consisted of 'a few rude dwellings of the ferry men'. Benn also suggests that the raths in the Belfast area bear testimony to a Danish presence and influence. This is unlikely, however, for while the Danes did indeed occupy parts of Ireland, in many cases intermarrying and adopting the language and customs of the native Irish, for example in 1182 Donald O Laghlin was king of Dal Riada and his name, *i mbéarla,* means the son of the Scandinavian, Francis Josph Bigger says of the forts:

> You hear these remains commonly called Danes' forts, now this is misleading for the Danes never built the earthworks that are scattered so broadcast over our county . . . the ex-

pression however may be a corruption of the
name of a primitive tribe that did build such
dwellings, namely the Tuatha - de -Danaan,
who occupied the land previous to the introduction of Christianity and whose name
may have become corrupted.

These forts and raths, regardless of their origins, were
fairly numerous in the Belfast area and from the evidence they
provide it seems that the district was amply inhabited by an in-
dustrious race of people, accomplished in the art of building
and gathered in small colonies throughout County Antrim and
around the Lagan and Farset rivers.

In 1177 the province of Ulster was granted to John de
Courcy by the English monarch on condition that he conquer
it. This he dutifully attempted to do, erecting a chain of castles
to defend the east Antrim coastline and living in the one he built
at Carrickfergus. He also built a small castle at Belfast to com-
mand the ford across the Lagan. Not surprisingly, all this
construction work aroused the wrath of the native Irish, and
Belfast was the scene of many pitched battles between the
dispossessed Irish and the English.

In 1315 a Scottish invasion by Edward Bruce caused
prolonged fighting between the Anglo-Normans, Scots and
native Irish and the castle at Belfast changed hands several
times until 1333 when there was a further Irish resurgence
which successfully swept all before it and pushed the English into a tiny pocket of east Ulster. The remainder of the area, including Belfast, was firmly outside the English Pale and was to
stay in Irish hands for two centuries with only Carrickfergus accepting the authority of the English Crown. Around this time
Hugh Boy O'Neill controlled the parish of Belfast and the name
of the area was changed from Dal Riada to North or Lower
Clandeboye (from the Irish *Clann Aoidh Buí*).

Sir John Davies, an Englishman serving in Ireland at
that time and later the Irish Attorney-General, described it
thus:

Assuredly in Ulster the sept of Hugh Boy
O'Neill then possessing Glenconkeyn and
Killeightra in Tyrone took the opportunity and
passing over the Bann did first expel the

English out of the Barony of Tuscard, which is now called the Rout and likewise out of the Glynnes and other lands up as far as Knockfergus which country or extent of land is at this time called the Lower Clann Hugh Boy. And shortly after that they came up into the Great Ardes, which the Latin writers call *Altitudines Ultoniae,* and was then the inheritance of the Savages by whom they were valiantly resisted for divers years but at last, for want of castles and fortifactions — for the saying of Henry Savage mentioned in every story is very memorable, that a castle of bones was better than a castle of stones — the English were overrun by the multitude of the Irishry.

During the next two centuries while Belfast castle remained in the hands of the native Irish, its residents changed occasionally as the result of inter-clan warfare and it was destroyed twice, once in 1503 and again in 1512 by the Earl of Kildare.

However by the 1550s the English were beginning to re-exert themselves — dissolving monasteries and their like — and although Belfast castle was 'granted' in 1552 to Conn Mac Neil Óg in return for his submission to Edward VI, a customary arrangement at that time by which hostilities were terminated, the English were merely marking time. In 1553, the Lord Chancellor, Cusacke, in a letter to the Duke of Northumberland gave the following covetous description of the greater Belfast area:

The country of (lower) Clandeboye is woods and bogs for the greatest part, wherein lie Knockfergus (Carrickfergus) and so to Glynnes where the Scots do inhabit. . . . Hugh (O'Neill) hath two castles one called Bealeforst, an old castle standing upon a ford that leadeth from Arde to Clanne Boye, which being well repaired, being now broken, would be a good defence between the woods and Knockfergus; the other called Castell Rioughe (Castlereagh) is four miles from Bealefarst, and standeth upon the plain in the midst of the woods of the Dufferin.

Even at that stage, strategic considerations to one side, the resources of timber (for shipbuilding) were too great a temptation for English entrepreneurs and so in 1567 Belfast castle was back in English hands once again. The following year a settlement was agreed between Brian Mac Phelim O'Neill of Clandeboye and Sir Henry Sidney, the English Lord Deputy, at a meeting in Belfast. They arranged, in return for assistance from O'Neill in developing the area around Belfast castle, to transfer the castle itself back to the O'Neill clan.

Totally disregarding this, a few years later, in 1571, Queen Elizabeth I granted Belfast castle and other O'Neill lands in Antrim and Down to Sir Thomas Smith, her secretary and to Thomas Smith, his son, which as Cathal O'Byrne records

> shows in quite simple language how easy it was in the good old days to 'grant' and give away what didn't belong to you.

The native Irish chieftains, especially the O'Neills, reacted angrily to this news. In fact so blatant was the double-cross that a Captain Piers (who had originally taken Belfast castle, in 1567, for the Crown), wrote to the Lord Deputy warning of the consequences of such a move. The Lord Deputy in turn warned that Smith's 'grant will bring the Irish into a knot to rebel'.

Thus, before the end of the year the native Irish were again in open revolt. Undeterred, Queen Elizabeth, in 1573, made a new grant of land in Ulster (including some which she had previously granted to Smith!) to Walter Devereux, the Earl of Essex. While Smith's reign was largely ineffectual, and his son was killed early in the campaign, Essex was a much more forceful and treacherous adversary intent upon building 'a corporate town' at Belfast because it was 'armed with all commodities as a principal haven, wood and good ground standing also upon a border and a place of great importance for service'. He also planned to build a bridge across the Lagan, plus barracks and stables together with a brewhouse, storehouse and a mill.

After some initial skirmishing he and Brian Mac Phelim O'Neill came to terms and indeed O'Neill offered to assist in building Belfast town. In this relaxed atmosphere Essex was invited by O'Neill to stay in Belfast castle. He accepted the invitation and then made Belfast castle the scene for the massacre of his host and all his people. As the Four Masters record:

> Peace, sociality and friendship were established between Brian, the son of Phelim Bacagh O'Neill, and the Earl of Essex, and a feast was afterwards prepared by Brian to which the Lord Justice and the chiefs of his people were invited and they passed three nights and days together pleasantly and cheerfully. At the expiration of this time, when they were agreeably drinking and making merry, Brian, his brother, and his wife were seized upon by the Earl, and all his people put unsparingly to the sword — men, women, youths and maidens — in Brian's own presence. Brian was afterwards sent to Dublin, together with his wife and brother, where they were cut in quarters. Such was the end of their feast. This unexpected massacre; this wicked and treacherous murder of the lord of the race of Hugh Boy O'Neill, the head and senior of the race of Eoghan, son of Niall of the Nine Hostages, and of all the Gaels, was a sufficient cause of hatred, of the English to the Irish.

Essex died in Dublin in 1576 before his plans to develop Belfast could be completed and a relative peace settled over the area as Elizabeth proceeded no further with her conquest. However, in 1595, as the English again began to encroach on his property Hugh O'Neill, the Earl of Tyrone, rose up in rebellion. He was successful in the early stages but by 1599 the tide began to turn with the arrival of Sir Arthur Chichester and Lord Mountjoy.

Chichester, who is regarded by many as the real founder of Belfast, first came to Ireland when he had to flee from Devonshire because of his involvement in the highway robbery of one of his queen's tax collectors. He remained in hiding for a short time in Ireland, before escaping to France, where he enlisted as a mercenary in the French service. His record there and his friends in high places reminded Elizabeth that such a man was sorely needed to sort out the rebellious Irish of Ulster. She gave him a pardon for his earlier indiscretion and a mandate for future criminality, and dispatched him to Ireland.

Here, he and Mountjoy, using famine and terror of every kind, carried out Elizabeth's policy of exterminating the native Irish with ruthlessness and obvious relish:

> I burned all along the lough within four miles of Dungannon and killed 100 people, sparing none of whatever quality, age or sex, soever besides many burned to death. We kill man, woman and child, horse, beast and whatsoever we find.

H. A. MacCartan wrote:

> Antrim and Down is a burning shambles, the wayside strewn with dead bodies of human beings whose lips are still green with the juices of grass on which they have been endeavouring to sustain life, women about a great fire in a wood cooking the bodies of slain children, O'Hanlon of Armagh exiled, O'Doherty's sister stripped naked in the wood and dead in childbirth, MacMahon hanged at his own door, Ulster of the trees and waving cornfields a lost and howling wilderness.

Hugh O'Neill was forced to surrender in 1603 and Chichester was granted some of his land including the castle of Belfast. The power of the Ulster chiefs was broken and their lands, the last in Ireland to be conquered, were now open to the English. Until this, as Chichester remarked, the lands controlled by the Ulster chieftains 'before these last wars, like the kingdom of China, were inaccessible to strangers'.

In 1607, the Flight of the Earls saw the final collapse of the Ulster chieftains and the way was cleared for wholesale plantation. As Chichester said at the time:

There was never a fairer opportunity offered to
any of his highness's predecessors to plant and
reform that rude and irreligious corner of the
North, than by the flight of the traitorous Earls
Tyrone and Tyreconnell with their co-partners
and adherents.

In 1608 the last of the O'Neills lost control of his territory. Conn O'Neill, who continued to reside in his castle at
Castlereagh, had earlier been the principal proprietor of an
area including the plains of Belfast, which incorporated the
meadows of the Falls. A number of Scottish courtiers of King
James I, who were greedy for land, felt 'that Ireland must be
the stage to act upon, it being unsettled, and many fortified
lands thereon altogether wasted, they concluded to push for for-
tunes in that kingdom.'

They seized their opportunity when Conn 'in a grand
debauch' at Castlereagh sent servants to bring more wine from
Belfast. Conn's men were attacked and after a fierce battle between them and the *'Bodach Sasanagh* soldiers' at Ballynafeigh
(the town of the playing fields) Conn was lodged in Carrickfergus castle on the charge of levying war against the
English monarch. He was rescued from Carrickfergus and
subsequently pardoned by King James but in return had to give
up his land to one Hugh Montgomery and his cohorts who had
contrived his arrest and arranged both his rescue and pardon.
Subsequently most of Conn's land in north Down and south
Antrim was planted with Scottish Presbyterians.

In 1611 Chichester had fortified and strengthened the
garrison in Belfast Castle and the town itself was becoming a
colonial settlement, 'plotted out in good form' and inhabited
mainly by English, Scottish and Manxmen.

In 1612 the whole 'parish of Belfast' was granted by
King James to Chichester. He continued with the plantation of
the area, the English colonies being added to by Scottish
planters who arrived in great numbers from the beginning of
James's reign. In the Belfast area the remaining Irish families
were pushed back to the south-western parts of the district,
mainly above Hannahstown. As George Benn records:

They are in general the poorest inhabitants, in-
considerable in number and yet most deserving

of notice, as being perhaps some of those whose progenitors once possessed the rich and fertile plains which lie below them.

Because these native or Gaelic Irish were forbidden to live within town or city walls, those who wished to live near Belfast gathered to a large extent outside the earth walls to the west, which were built after the 1641 rebellion in the general area of what is now Castle Street. These walls had disappeared by the early eighteenth century. The castle built by Sir Arthur Chichester was situated at the corner of what is now Donegall Place and took in all of the modern Castle Place, Cornmarket, Arthur Street and Donegall Place; and its gardens, lawns and bowling green stretched to the Lagan river and away to the woods at Cromac and Stranmillis. In 1666, what is now Belfast city centre was a green garden with orchards, fish ponds and cherry gardens. In 1708 the castle was burnt down and not rebuilt and its gardens were gradually taken over for commercial development.

According to tradition, the old Falls Road ran from Derriaghy to the foot of High Street. It was a country lane, a cow track with the main coach road to Dublin going down Durham Street and through Sandes Row — now Sandy Row. The present Falls Road met the old road at Maryburn Lane, above Milltown, then close to a cornmill. Callendar's Fort stood on what is now the Glen Road, on the left going from town where the road rises before the turn at St Teresa's Chapel. It was known also to be the site of an old church and graveyard, and the word Callendar is probably a corruption of the Irish word, *calluragh,* meaning an old graveyard. The area now known as Andersonstown was called Whitesidestown because of the small colony of people called Whiteside who lived there. According to Cathal O'Byrne these people were prominent in the 1798 rebellion and one of them turned his coat, changed to the government side and dispossessed the others. The Lake Glen area once contained a lake with a *crannóg* (lake dwelling) in its centre; and an old fort in the vicinity gave its name to the townland of Ballydownfine, i.e. *Baile Dún Fionn,* the townland of the white fort. The fort is also commemorated in the name of a nearby pub, The White Fort Inn.

From the point where the present Falls Road met the old road it turned through what is now the cemetery — once a brickfield — crossing in front of the industrial school — in more recent times *An Cumann Beag* and the 'Old Felons'. This circuitous route avoided a high ridge which is still to be seen from the Falls Park at the bus depot just below the R.U.C. barracks at the present junction of the Falls, Glen and Andersonstown Roads. The bus station was once the site of a barracks for a British Army cavalry regiment which was garrisoned there. From the industrial school the old road cuts off a corner of the park up through the high ground of the City Cemetery and Glenalina, and crossed the Whiterock Road above MacRory Park, where the Brits have erected their Fort Pegasus. Long ago Whiterock was known as Kill Pipers' Hill and a little fort on the north side of MacRory Park was said to be the fort of the pipers.

Interestingly enough, when the British Army sappers were building Fort Pegasus a few years ago the timbers at the north side parallel to Britton's Parade persisted in collapsing. At the time, older people in the Whiterock area recalled a story of a fairy fort at that point and the fairies got the credit for the demolitions. The British Army blamed it on high winds, but one never knows. They have been known to tell lies about things like that.

The old road then made its way through what was later the Brickfields (now Springhill), on by the old cotton mill — once the site of a great fort which gave its name to the Forth river — and through Springfield village to the Shankill. Here it continued down to Bower's Hill and Peter's Hill to the north gate of the city at the upper end of Goose Lane (now North Street) and into the city centre. The Shankill Road gets its name from the Irish *an sean cill* — the old church — said to have been founded by St Patrick; and the Springfield Road was so called because wells or springs of water, so important later to the linen industry, came from beneath the ground at that point. The limestone band which runs along the Black Mountain gives the Whiterock Road its name. This limestone also purified the water and on the sites in the Falls area where wells of particularly high quality water emerged several mineral water companies were later established.

Townsend Street marked the end of Belfast town and Mill Street, now Divis Street, was the site of a mill, probably built in 1575 by the Earl of Essex, who wrote to Queen Elizabeth I in that year that 'the brewhouse, a storehouse and mill at Belfast are completed'. At the junction of Barrack Street and Mill Street, Watson's public house was the place where the toll or custom was collected on farm produce coming into town from Ballinderry, Glenavy, Hannahstown and Upper Falls. Barrack Street was the site of a barracks built in 1737 and the scene of much activity around 1798 when the United Irishmen were greatly sought after by the raiding soldiers. At the junction of Pound Street and Barrack Street a plot of low ground enclosed by a stone wall was reserved as a cattle and dog pound. A clear stream of water ran through the pound and from this the Pound Loney area got its name, *lonn* being the Irish for 'swift water'. Incidentally, Dinneen's Irish/English dictionary also explains *lonnan* as 'a grassy recess running up into high basaltic cliffs', and it is from this, the Black Mountain being basalt, that we get the name 'the mountain lonnan' between New Barnsley and Dermott Hill estates. A further meaning comes from the Scots dialect word for a lane 'loanan' or 'loaning' which is commonly used in counties Antrim and Down.

In 1783 the first Catholic chapel was built, close to the pound in Chapel Lane, and was rebuilt in 1868. Previously, Mass had been celebrated in the open air in the old graveyard at Friar's Bush and afterwards in a disused shed behind a house in Castle Street. Before this, priests, on the run and unregistered, had attended in secret to the spiritual needs of their congregation.

In fact in 1708 one Phelim O'Hamill, 'popish priest of Belfast, Derriaghy and Drum' was arrested and remained in Belfast prison until he died. Rewards were offered for information leading to the arrest and conviction of unregistered Catholic clergymen: £20 for a priest and £50 for an archbishop or bishop.

During this period, a local administrator was able to boast:

> Thank God we are not under any great fears here, for upon this occasion I had made the constable return me a list of all inhabitants within this town, and we have not among us above seven papists, and by the return made by the high constable, there is not above 150 papists in the whole barony.

A later report stated that 'no popish headmaster or any

headmistress keeps a school within the county of Antrim.'

With the development of Belfast in the 1750s and a dramatic increase in the Catholic population, the need for an alternative to the old shed in Castle Street as a place of worship was keenly felt by the Church authorities. In 1768 a Fr Hugh O'Donnell succeeded in obtaining a thirty-one year lease of an old building at the back of the houses opposite Marquis Street on the south side of Mill Street. Entrance to this temporary chapel was via the aptly named Squeeze-Gut Alley. For fifteen years this building was used as a place of worship by Belfast Catholics until Fr O'Donnell secured a lease for a term of seventy-one years of premises in Crooked Lane, now Chapel Lane, for the 'Congregation of Roman Catholics'. This longer lease had been secured because of a certain freedom extended to Catholics in 1779 when in place of the clause limiting them to lease of any premises for thirty-three years, they were permitted to obtain leases 'not exceeding 999 years'.

In 1784 old St Mary's was completed and the tolerance, at least among some sections of the population, towards Catholics was indicated by the presence at the opening ceremony of the first Belfast company of the Volunteers, Presbyterians all, who had contributed towards the cost of the new church and provided a guard of honour at the opening ceremony.

With their own chapel, the Catholic population began to increase and although Thomas Gaffikin was to describe the Pound Loney as having been in 1825, 'just a few houses around a cattle pound and dog kennel on the north side of Barrack Street', the next few decades saw a marked change in both the appearance and population of the area of *Tuath na bhFál*, or the 'district of the high hedges'.

Tuath na BhFál

The hedges they all grew around
Grew around, grew around
The hedges they all grew around
A long time ago.
Belfast Street Song

IN the old days the Farset river ran from the hills above the Falls Road and formed a mill dam beside the flour mill at what is now Percy Street. It continued from there to a spot opposite Durham Street where it divided to flow through the Pound, with the main section continuing down through Millfield to turn the wheel of the old manor mill and run through Bank Lane and High Street before joining the Lagan. The river took its name from the sand banks at the ford on the Lagan somewhere near Anne Street, and it is from there that Belfast or *Béal Feirste* — 'the mouth of the ford of the sand banks' — gets its name.

The present Falls area was known then as *Tuath na bhFál*, the district of the high hedges, and the Falls Road was *Bóthar na bhFál*, the 'road of the high hedges'. It was a country lane with meadows and cornfields stretching, according to

Cathal O'Byrne, from Millfield to Ballygomartin and Carr's Glen, with the hills 'cultivated almost to the top'. Change, however, was on its way and the area of *Tuath na bhFál*, with its green fields and meadows, slowly gave way to new houses and factories.

By 1812 the population had increased to 4,000 and by 1861 it was 40,000. This dramatic increase, which particularly afected the Loney area, was due to a number of factors, not least the development of the linen industry and the subsequent rise and growth of industrial Belfast. Linen, for long made by the farming communities of Antrim and Down for domestic use, was often exported to England by merchants who bought surplus cloth from the farmers at local fairs. It was a saleable commodity, and with little or no competition in England it fetched a good price.

The manufacturing of linen was, however, slow and tedious especially the final process of bleaching. The brown linen was bleached in the open air, usually for a period of about six weeks. Early in the eighteenth century the merchants began to buy the brown linen from the farmers and to bleach it themselves; and many bleaching greens were established around the town. To meet the requirements of this new trade Belfast port began expanding, and linen started its growth as a major industry. Indeed in the 1780s the White Linenhall, forerunner of the present City Hall, was built.

Soon, newly invented factory machinery was imported from England, but because this new machinery could not spin or weave fine linen thread, the manufacture of linen continued mainly as a cottage industry and was replaced to some extent by cotton which the Belfast merchants imported along with coal for use in their new cotton mills. By 1811 there were thirty-three of these new mills in Belfast and the industry boomed during the Napoleonic Wars when cloth was needed for soldiers' uniforms. Water was required to drive the machinery and to process the cloth, and factories lined the banks of the small rivers running down behind the Falls Road.

The first cotton mill in Ireland was built by Robert Joy, Thomas McCabe and Captain J. McCracken. The McCrackens are famous in their own right but it is interesting that McCabe was responsible, in 1786, for stopping an attempt by Belfast merchants to embark on the slave trade. When asked by one Waddel Cunningham to sign a contract for the proposed

Belfast Slave-Ship Company he startled onlookers in the old Belfast Exchange by replying:

> 'May God wither the hand and consign the name to eternal infamy of the man who will sign that document.'

The scheme fell through.

After the Napoleonic Wars, the cotton industry in both England and Belfast slumped, but in 1825 a method of 'wet spinning' solved the problems of spinning the linen flax. The linen industry came into its own and, with flax being grown at home and linen facing less competition than cotton, the Belfast factory owners seized their opportunity to expand this trade. By 1838 there were only three or four cotton mills left and the flax mills had increased to fifteen. By 1850 there were thirty-six mills, employing over 33,000 people.

With the expansion of the linen industry, the population of the Falls area increased; the majority of new residents were attracted by the prospect of employment, coming to Belfast from rural areas where large families found it difficult to eke out a living on the land. In the 1830s when the factories changed to linen spinning, effectively killing the cottage industry, numerous handloom weavers flocked to the mills for jobs and finally, during the potato blight of 1845 to 1849, many families impoverished by the famine moved into Belfast city. The poor were most adversely affected by these developments; Catholics, being the majority of that class, provided a cheap unskilled labour force for the mills, and they flocked into the Falls area.

They went in smaller numbers to other areas of Belfast, notably the Markets and Carrick Hill/New Lodge; by the early nineteenth century these areas had small but well-defined Catholic populations. As late as 1825 there were few houses in the Falls district. With the exception of the distillery near where Wordie's haulage firm later stood, no more dwellings existed that side of the road up to Clowney Bridge except a curds and cream shop opposite Charter's Mill and a small house facing the present Beehive Bar. The Grosvenor Road and Albert Street were rough country roads and around Gordon's Mill, later Grieve's, was a gooseberry garden. Between Albert Street and Leeson Street was Margaret Connolly's field, and a cluster of white cottages stood facing Northumberland Street. There were a few houses dotted about the area, and a large flax pond on what was to become McDonnell Street, around which blackberries grew in abundance. The cottages at the corner of what was later Albert Street were called Bogan's Row, and lower down the road were the Half-Bap and Waxey's fields.

In 1850 the then Marquis of Donegall died, leaving his estate heavily in debt. He owned most of the land around the Loney and Falls area and his estate was sold off to anyone with money to buy. Some of it was bought for industrial development but many of the mill owners began to build homes for their workers. By 1861 the streets of the old Pound Loney (demolished in the 1970s) were built. Mill Street was renamed Divis Street, and new streets had appeared between Cullingtree Road, Milford Street and Pound Street. These included English Street, Bow Street, Scotch Street, Irwin Street, Quadrant Street and Albert Street. Carmel Gallagher, in *All Around the Loney O,* shows the similarity of the direction of the field boundaries at that time and the streets which were erected on them. The Loney and the Falls area as we know it were beginning to emerge from the green fields and grassy meadows of *Tuath na bhFál.* Mills lined the right hand side of the Falls Road and the road itself was developed as a main route for traffic bringing raw and finished material to and from the mills.

The houses provided for the residents of this area, in keeping with the general conditions of working people, were miserable in the extreme. They were as small as possible, their yards had no exits or alleyways at the rear and there were no toilets, all sewage and refuse having to come through the front door. In 1852, 7,000 out of 10,000 houses had to rely for water on public fountains, pumps or water carts. The small overcrowded houses and the insanitary and polluted water supply earned Belfast the highest death rate from typhoid in both Ireland and Britain until 1898. There were also recurrent epidemics of cholera and typhus which claimed the lives of thousands.

In 1865 a bye-law was passed that all new streets were to be properly paved and sewered before occupation but even this basic necessity was a long time being implemented, and by the time regulations governing the structural quality and size of the houses were passed in 1889 the vast majority of houses in the old Falls area were already built. All were without inside toilets, hot water or baths. The Falls Baths, opened in 1894, provided

Back yards.

such necessities. Insult was added to injury when Dunville Park was presented to the citizens of Belfast by the Belfast whiskey family Dunville in memory of their sister. It was complete with toilets and washrooms — 'where the working class may learn the art of cleanliness'. This situation remained unchanged until recent times when home improvements were made, not by the housing authorities but by the residents themselves. In fact, domestic electric lighting did not come to many parts of the area until the 1950s. I vividly recall our next door neighbour getting her electricity put in and can remember other houses, like hers, which were dependent on gas mantles or paraffin lamps for their lighting.

Despite their lack of facilities, the 'new' houses were considered by those who lived in them as an improvement on the houses they had previously occupied. They were also in what could have been described as a suburb of the town and had the temporary advantage of being surrounded by countryside and fresh air. Whether these factors outweighed the drawbacks it is difficult to say, but soon the small houses in the back streets were overcrowded with people, with whole families sleeping in single rooms as cousins and in-laws sought shelter near the mills.

This dramatic increase in the Catholic population was the cause of some concern to the Church authorities who feared that 'only one in every three Belfast Catholics were attending Sunday Mass'. One obvious reason for such widespread absenteeism was that St Mary's Church in Chapel Lane could not cope with the size of the congregation now living in the Falls area. Old St Mary's Chapel was scarcely half the size of the present one and could seat only about 150 people. Although the present church was built in 1868 as an extension to the old one, lack of building land restricted its size and it was obvious that a larger site was required to deal with the huge congregation.

Some of St Mary's original congregation said their prayers in Irish, especially the 'Fadyees' (Paddies) or fish dealers, who came from Omeath and lived close to St Mary's where they made up a small Irish-speaking colony.

The problem of securing a suitable site for a large church was solved by one Bernard Hughes, owner of Hughes's Bakery, famous for 'Barney Hughes's Baps'. He obtained in 1858, from John Alexander of Milford, a large area of land which extended 214 feet along Milford Street, 138 feet along Dysart Street, 138 feet along Derby Street and 197 feet along Alexander Street West. The local bishop was granted this land by Bernard Hughes for a nominal rent and soon work began on the building of a new Catholic church to serve the Pound Loney and Falls Road.

This new church, St Peter's Pro-Cathedral, was opened on 14 October 1866, minus its present spires which were not erected until 1885. The dedication and opening were described by the *Belfast Morning News* as 'the most imposing in connection with the Roman Catholic Church which has ever taken place in Belfast'.

Admittance to the ceremony was by ticket only, with quite exhorbitant prices being charged, and special excursion parties travelled from Cookstown, Moneymore, Magherafelt, Castledawson, Toomebridge and Randalstown. Twelve bishops, including the Cardinal, were in the congregation, as were many Protestants who contributed generously to the collection. A total of £2,260 was collected and St Peter's, the first church in Belfast to be built in Gothic style, commenced to

Saint Peter's Church

serve the spiritual needs of the people of the Pound Loney and the Falls area.

For their part most of the congregation were devout and conscientious Catholics, rising early to receive holy communion on 'the nine first Fridays' before commencing work in the mills, and establishing a practice in other Belfast churches where, as Bishop Henry reported in 1896, 'we are compelled to begin the communions at half past four in the morning in order that those present may get to their work at six o'clock'.

St. Peter's was also to provide the inspiration for the 'Pioneer Total Abstinence Association of the Sacred Heart'. This arose when a visiting priest, Fr Cullen, decided in 1889 to ask parishioners to take a life-long pledge to abstain from alcohol. Before this the practice had been to give the pledge to the entire congregation, especially after a temperance mission. Obviously, such a random undertaking wasn't very successful, but to Fr Cullen's surprise when he called for volunteers for the life-long pledge, over 300 men and women publicly announced their acceptance. Despite this, it goes without saying that the street corner public houses, dotted throughout the area, have long enjoyed a profitable trade.

The Union and the Unions

I am a good old workingman
Each day I carry a wee tin can
A large penny bap and a clipe of ham
I am a good old working man.
Belfast Street Song

ALTHOUGH the people of West Belfast were a minority in the city as a whole, the increase of the Catholic population was more marked than that of any other section of the populace. This dramatic increase provided fuel for those who stoked the fires of sectarian bitterness so that, as the Belfast linen industry continued to develop and ancillary industries such as engineering, brickmaking, shipbuilding and rope-making sprang up, every effort was made to ensure that skilled jobs and management positions did not fall to Catholic workers. These efforts, part of a policy aimed at dividing the working people and protecting the ascendancy position of the unionist class, were hugely successful in that the majority of the Falls Road people were employed at cheap rates in the mills which stretched from the Springfield Road to Northumberland Street — the Blackstaff, Milford's, Ross's, Grieve's, Craig's, Charter's,

Kennedy's and the Durham Street Weaving Company.

It was women and children who worked in these mills, while men were generally employed as unskilled workers, carters or building labourers. Because of the consistently high level of male unemployment (a permanent feature of life in West Belfast) women, with regular work in the mills, became the breadwinners. They were employed for a minimum wage, slaving from 6.30 a.m. to 6.00 p.m. on weekdays with a break for breakfast at 8.00 a.m. and a dinner break at 1.00 p.m.; on Saturdays work stopped at noon. The flax had to go through nine different processes, all extremely dangerous to the workers' health; and for this the women at the turn of the century earned some eight shillings a week.

The millworkers had various names, usually a description of the job they did — doffers, weavers, reelers, flax-roughers, rovers, scutchers, band-tiers, spinners, tenters and winders. They also had their own class system as the following verses illustrate:

Oh, my name is Rosie Mullan
I'm a doffer in the mill
My boyfriend doesn't know it
And I hope he never will
For if he gets to know it
He would drop me on the spot
And that would never do
Because I love him a hell of a lot.

*   *   *

Do you want to breed a fight?
We are the Rovers!
For it's if you want to breed a fight
Oh, we are the Jolly Fine Rovers.

*   *   *

Twenty doffers in a room, oh but they were cosy
They sang so sweet so very, very sweet
That they charmed the heart of the band-tier O
The band-tier O, the band-tier O
The lovely blue-eyed band tier O.

*   *   *

Oh, do you know her or do you not?
This new doffing mistress that we have got
Oh Agnes Savage is her name   .
And she hangs her coat upon the highest frame
Ra-de-ri-fle-ra, ra-de-ri-fle-ree.

Oh, Monday morning when she comes in
She hangs her coat upon the highest pin
She turns around for to view her girls
Saying 'Damn you doffers, lay up your ends'
Ra-de-ri-fle-ra, ra-de-ri-fle-ree.

Children, mostly girls, worked for the same hours as the adults, until new legislation in 1874 introduced an arrangement whereby one week they worked three days and went to school the other two, and the following week the balance was reversed. These children were called half-timers. In 1891 the minimum age for millworkers was raised to eleven and in 1901 to twelve. Half-timers in the years 1904 to 1907 were paid 3s. 4½ d. for the 'long week' and 2s. 11½ d. for the 'short week'.

The working conditions in the mills were worse even than the living conditions in the small back streets. In the spinning rooms the uncomfortably hot air was kept damp to prevent the fine linen thread from breaking, and in the earlier stages of the process the very air in the carding or spinning rooms was thick with fine 'pouce' or dust which came from the raw flax. The millworkers and especially the doffers, who worked bare-footed, inhaled this pouce and serious bronchial illness was common. The death rate from tuberculosis was also very high, with the result that the greater number of these workers died before the age of forty-five and children were generally small and badly developed. In 1897 an outbreak of typhoid affected some 27,000 people. Long hours in such conditions and an inadequate diet of tea, buttermilk, potatoes, herrings, cheap cuts of meat and a variety of homebaked bannocks and farls did little to alleviate such consistent ill-health.

In 1909, Dr Bailie, City Medical Officer of Health, stated in an official report:

> Premature births were found to be most prevalent among women who worked in the

mills and factories, engaged in such work as the following — spinning, weaving, machining, tobacco-spinning and laundry work. Many of the women appear to be utterly unable for such work owing to the want of sufficient nourishment and suitable clothing and being through stress of circumstances compelled to work to the date of confinement would be accountable for the many young and delicate children found by the Health Visitors.

Dr Bailie also recorded:

As in previous years it is found that consumption is most prevalent among the poor, owing largely to the unfavourable conditions under which necessity compels them to live such as dark, ill-ventilated houses and insanitary habits together with insufficient food and clothing.

A Belfast street song still heard today reflects on that period and on how marriage provided a possible, if temporary, escape.

Wallflower, wallflower, growing up so high,
All the little children are all going to die,
All except for Kathy McKay for she's the only one,
She can dance, she can sing,
She can show her wedding ring.

The working régime in the mills was extremely harsh. If you were late, you lost a day's work with the subsequent hardship caused by the loss of wages. The workers were summoned to their toil by the penetrating screech of the millhorn which wakened the slumbering populace at 5.00 a.m. In many streets a 'rapper-upper' ensured that no one slept in, and soon the streets were black with throngs of noisy, cheerful mill-workers.

Five o'clock the horn does blow,
Half-past five, we all must go,
If you be a minute late,

Oul Jack Horn will shut the gate,
So early in the morning.

The women were unorganised, as were most of the
working people, and any attempt to improve conditions or
assert their right to belong to trade unions met with united opposition from the employers. There had been some attempts to
organise mill-workers at the turn of the century but one of the
first concerted efforts to organise trade unions among unskilled
workers — unions for tradesmen and craftsmen existed in
Belfast to some degree from 1788 — came in 1907 when James
Larkin arrived in Belfast as organiser for the National Union of
Dock Labourers.

While this did not initially have any direct effect on the
people of the Falls Road, it is worth looking briefly at Larkin's
efforts to organise a trade union for dock labourers, carters and
coal fillers at Belfast docks. For a brief period sectarian divisions were set aside and working people united into an effective
labour movement. This unity was met by the combined opposition of the employers and the civil authorities, in most cases one
and the same people, and by the R.I.C. and British Army. The
unionist press, politicians and employers did their utmost to
undermine Larkin's influence by denouncing him as 'a
socialist and a Catholic' and by warning Protestant workers not
to join the labour agitations. In May a lockout of union men at
Belfast docks led to a strike which quickly spread to other
workplaces when blackleg and scab labour was imported from
Liverpool by the employers.

Thousands of extra R.I.C. and British soldiers were
drafted into the city to protect the strike-breakers and the
employers stated that 'no person representing any trade union
or combination' would be recognised by them, that they would
exercise the right to employ or dismiss whom they chose, and
that if a strike took place without three days' written notice the
strikers would be locked out and their jobs given to others.
Every worker who wanted his job back was given until 15 July
to sign a document accepting these conditions. The document
was rejected.

The workers remained united, despite frenzied efforts
by the establishment to divide them, especially during the mad
month of July, and those on strike were supported by other
workers, including the Belfast Trades Council, the Belfast

branches of the Amalgamated Society of Carpenters and Join-
ers, the Belfast railwaymen and the linen workers. Larkin's
efforts were also supported by the Dungannon Clubs, a literary
and debating front for the Irish Republican Brotherhood (I.R.B.)
whose prominent members in Belfast included Denis McCullogh,
Bulmer Hobson, Robert Lynd and Seán Mac Diarmada.

By the end of July the strike involved 2,500 dockers, coal
fillers and carters and had even spread to the ranks of the
R.I.C. The near mutiny in that force, despite the dismissal of
the chief spokesman, Constable Barrett, and the transfer of
other dissidents, forced the government to improve pay and
conditions for R.I.C. men.

In August, in an effort to provoke sectarian violence, extra troops were stationed in West Belfast with the express purpose of provoking clashes between them and local people. Parts
of the Falls were cordoned off and residents were stopped, sear-
ched and questioned. This harassment led to demonstrations
and riots until, on 12 August, the troops opened fire on a crowd
of Catholics assembled on the Grosvenor Road. Two people
were killed and many others were seriously injured. Larkin,
who was on the Falls Road during this period, denounced, with
local labour leaders, the presence of British troops in such force
in the Falls area when the strike was taking place in another part
of the town; but the unionist newspapers used the shooting to
portray the labour agitation as 'part of a conspiracy against the
unionist cause in Ireland'.

The British trade union leaders became alarmed and
rushed to Belfast where they commenced talks with the
employers without any consultation with Larkin. They agreed
on a pay increase and on the right of the employers to employ
non-union labour. The strike ended on 28 August and Larkin
was later to claim that the men were forced back by the unions'
refusal to continue paying them strike pay. Although the
alliance of Protestant and Catholic workers only temporarily
united these divided sections of the working people it showed
very clearly what could be achieved if a permanent unity could
be forged; but it was also clear how remote, given the influence
of Orangeism, such a development really was within a society
dominated by the Orange ascendancy. In such an atmosphere
in 1911, a strike by Belfast's linen slaves commenced, organised largely by James Connolly and involving a minority of the
Falls Road mill workers.

The Linen Slaves of Belfast

There goes that bloody whistle
And you never get a stand
Sure you'd be better off in the Union
Or in Mac Namara's Band.

Belfast Millsong

AS we have seen, the women employed in the mills were poorly organised and the working régime was strict, with trade union spirit among the workers extremely low. Efforts by the labour leader James Larkin to organise the Belfast dock workers and carters into a united, if temporary, labour movement in 1907 had left the linen workers largely untouched, and by 1911 new rules forbidding singing or laughing were introduced in the mills. Women could be fined for such 'offences' or for fixing their hair during working hours, and the penalty for bringing a newspaper, darning or knitting needles to work was instant dismissal.

Into Belfast and the Falls Road came James Connolly. He had been invited back to Ireland, from America, by the Socialist Party of Ireland and promised £2 a week. He joined the newly formed Irish Transport and General Workers Union and in July 1911 he was appointed Ulster organiser and secretary. Moving to Belfast to take up the post, he had to split his family up amongst republican and socialist friends until he found a home to rent.

His £2 a week was paid infrequently so that his friends D. R. Campbell, Danny McDevitt and Joe Mitchell pawned their gold watches to pay the first instalment of rent and buy groceries. The house was at 1 Glenalina Terrace, now 420 Falls Road, just below and opposite the City Cemetery, facing the Whiterock Road, and the family lived there until Good Friday 1916 when Mrs Connolly received word from her husband that they should join him in Dublin.

James Connolly set about the job of organising and winning recognition of the labour unions, especially in the docks, and was soon to turn his attention and his pen to the struggles of the mill workers. In October 1911 he wrote in the *Irish Worker:*

> The whole atmosphere of the mill is an atmosphere of slavery. The workers are harassed by petty bosses, mulcted in fines for the most trivial offences and robbed and cheated in a systematic manner. If a spinner whose weekly wage averaged 12s. 3d. lost a day's work, stayed out a day, she is fined 2s. 7d., a sum out of all proportion to her daily earnings. The same was true of half-timers and doffers.

Connolly also condemned the deplorable conditions in which the women worked:

> Imagine a spinning room so hot with a moist heat that all the girls and women must work in bare feet, with dress open at the breast and arms, hair tied up to prevent it irritating the skin . . . imagine the stifling, suffocating atmosphere that in a few months banishes the colour from the cheeks of the rosiest half-timer and reduces all to one common deathly pallor.

These conditions and the oppressive system of fines caused increasing frustration among the workers, but as only nine percent of them were members of trade unions and as the

The house where James Connolly lived from 1910 to 1916.

major union — the Linen Textile Operatives Society — did little except raise the issue at Belfast Trades Council, any industrial action seemed doomed to failure. To strike was to starve, and fear of the workhouse was a major deterrent for most of the linen workers.

At that time also the mill owners had agreed to limit production by fifteen percent. In practice, however, each manufacturer attempted to maintain production at the same level while working shorter hours. This was done by speeding up the machinery and thus increasing the work load upon the mill workers. They, frustrated by the lack of action from their own union leaders, soon turned to Connolly for help.

Nora Connolly O'Brien describes a meeting in Connolly's office in Corporation Street:

> 'Yes,' a woman near the fire was saying, her husky voice fierce and bitter, 'it's over forty-five years since I started working in the mills. I was just turned eight when I began. When you were eight you were old enough to work. Worked in the steam, making your rags all wet and sometimes up to your ankles in water. The older you got the more work you got. If you got married you kept on working. Your man didn't get enough for a family. You worked 'til your baby came and went back as soon as you could; and then, God forgive you! you counted the days 'til your child could be a half-timer and started the whole hell of a life over again.'

It wasn't long until the women were driven out on strike. On 4 October 1911 over 1,000 of them marched out of various mills and appealed to Connolly to lead them. He readily gave his support, although the Textile Operatives Society representatives refused to give theirs and advised the women not to strike. Without union funds to back them the women could draw only two shillings a week strike pay which they secured by street collections. Connolly wrote:

> The girls fought heroically. We held a meeting in St Mary's Hall and packed it with 3,000 girls and women. They were packed from floor to

ceiling, squatting on the floor between the plat-
form and the seats — 3,000 cheering, singing
enthusiastic females and not a hat among
them.

At such a meeting, at the Custom House steps, Nora Connolly
spoke in public for the first time.

The strike was essentially about conditions; while
Connolly had put a demand for higher pay he regarded this as a
negotiating point which could be given in return for an
improvement in working conditions so that 'should any girl feel
happy enough to sing, she can do so without any fear of losing
her job'. Yet despite all their efforts it soon became clear that
the strikers were being beaten by the lack of union funding,
some clerical opposition and the powerful position of the mill
owners. They were in no position to win their demands by
orthodox methods, and solidarity was crumbling. In fact, only
two mills were affected by the strike and neither of these —
York Street Flax Spinning Company and Milewater Mills —
were on the Falls Road. The majority of women were so
oppressed that Connolly's attempt to free 'the linen slaves' was
well-nigh impossible. The *Irish News* perhaps best summed up
the 'respectable' nationalist attitude when it offered the opinion
that

unorganised displays of this kind can lead to no
industrial gain for the workers and can only
serve to prejudice their position.

Furthermore, with a surplus of linen the mill-owners
could afford to lock out and starve the strikers while the Textile
Operatives Society, opposed to Connolly's republican views,
persistently attacked him. Two weeks after the strike began
Connolly proposed that the women commence a 'stay-in-
strike', one of the first examples of the use of this tactic in
Ireland. He advised the women to go back

but not in ones and twos, but gather outside
the mills and all go in in a body and go in singing. Defy every oppressive and unreasonable
rule. If one girls laughs and is reproved let
everyone laugh. If a girl is checked for singing

> let the whole room start singing at once and if anyone is dismissed, all should put on their shawls and march out. And when you are returning march in singing and cheering.

And so, in some cases at least, it came to be. One manager who sent a girl home had to send for her again. Work was resumed only when she returned and was welcomed back with a song. Though the strike had failed a moral victory was gained. About 300 doffers and spinners were organised into the Irish Textile Workers' Union, a section of the Irish Transport and General Workers' Union (I.T.G.W.U.) and Connolly helped them to satisfy their need for recreation by renting a small hall in the Falls Road as a club and engaging a fiddler and a teacher of Irish dancing. The women helped to pay for this by a small weekly subscription and all enjoyed 'the Mill Girls' Ball' which was held every year as well as an excursion to the country or seaside. And in return the mill girls made up a song about Connolly.

> Cheer up Connolly, your name is everywhere,
> You left old Baldy sitting in the chair,
> Crying for mercy, mercy wasn't there,
> So cheer up, Connolly, your name is everywhere.

Drawing largely on his Belfast experiences, Connolly, in December 1912, was to write of

> a discontented working class and a rebellious womanhood. I cannot separate these two great things in my mind. Every time the labourer, be it man or woman, secures a triumph in the battle for juster conditions, the mind of the labourer receives that impulse towards higher things that comes from the knowledge of power . . . the fruits of victory of the organised working class are as capable of being stated in terms of spiritual uplifting as in the material terms of cash.

And in *The Reconquest of Ireland* (1915) Connolly returned to the plight of the millworkers, vividly describing at length their working and living conditions and castigating the establishment.

> In these industrial parts of the North of Ireland
> the yoke of capitalism lies heavily upon the
> backs of the people. . . . In this part of Ireland
> the child is old before it knows what it is to be
> young. . . . In their wisdom our lords and
> masters often leave full grown men
> unemployed but they can always find use for
> the bodies and limbs of our children.

And so it was. And so too did the mills remain, outliving
the brave James Connolly by many years. Not for nothing did
we read little of such occurrences in our school history books.
We passed the mills every day, knowing little of the slavery
upon which they prospered. Instead we read about or were lec-
tured upon the shrewd business sense of the unionist landowning and manufacturing class and of how they built up the
North's textile industry. Yet the people whose sweated bodies
they sapped live all around us. My grandmother worked as a
half-timer. So undoubtedly did many of my readers' grandmothers, if they come from an industrial area. And it wasn't a
thousand years ago. Some readers will have worked in the mills
themselves, others have grandmothers, mothers or aunts who
were doffers or half-timers.

Connolly's house still stands, just up from St James's;
and now it bears a commemorative plaque which was donated,
to our shames, by one Gerry Fitt on behalf of the Republican
Labour Party. The Republican Labour Party, like Gerry Fitt's
republicanism, is no longer with us, but conditions in the mills
remained, generally speaking, unchanged until the 1940s. The
half-timer system ended in 1923 but attempts to win union
recognition and better wages did not succeed for many years.
By this time the linen industry was going through a period
of serious decline. In 1927 the industry, boasting the greatest
concentration of linen plants in the world, reached all-time
record levels of production, but by 1930 the number of
unemployed linen workers in Belfast was almost 20,000. For
the Belfast spinners and weavers there followed a series of
depressions and partial recoveries until by the summer of 1938
more than half the industry's labour force was unemployed. A

recovery was made after the war when the world shortage of textile products made these years profitable for the industry. By 1951, however, this backlog had been met: the linen industry was faced with a massive reduction in orders, and by July 1952 over 10,000 linen workers were unemployed.

On the Falls Road today only Ross's mill has survived; and it still operates a 'granny shift', or did until recently. The others have been demolished, burned out, or are used as warehouses. Until their closure, despite improvements in wages and working hours, the actual working conditions remained archaic. Mill buildings can still be seen today up Conway Street where one is used by the Conway Street Community Development complex. This worthy project, under the guidance of the radical Fr Des Wilson is endeavouring to provide social, economic, cultural and educational facilities for local people. Other mill buildings can be seen also in Sevastopol Street or down Broadway and on the Springfield Road and Cupar Street. Anyone passing, perhaps on the way to the dole, should take a dander round and have a look at them. But they should watch out for the ghosts as they rush back and forth, especially at tea times, to beat Jack Horn.

> You'll easy know a weaver
> When she comes into town
> With her oul greasy hair
> And her scissors hanging down
> With a shawl around her shoulders
> And a shuttle in her hand
> You'll easy know a weaver
> For she'll never get a man
> No, she'll never get a man
> No, she'll never get a man
> You'll easy know a weaver
> For she'll never get a man.

In 1969 I stood behind a barricade of burning tyres at the corner of Albert Street and watched petrol bombs showering into the mill at Northumberland Street. The enormity of it all frightened me a wee bit as the huge place began to blaze. I didn't really understand then what was burning. I know now. And so undoubtedly did the person who threw the first molotov.

Saints or Sinners?

Who is God
And where is God
Of whom is God
And where his dwelling?
Anon. Translated from the Irish by James Carney.

PROTESTANT churches in the Falls area outnumbered the Catholic ones up until the early 1960s and the current redevelopment of the area. Despite the overwhelming Catholic population it has long been a proud local boast that none of the Protestant congregations were ever molested or interfered with in any way.

The Protestant churches served various denominations. The Church of Ireland had three in the area. Christ Church, one of the oldest was established in 1833 in College Square North, and it gave to locals a saying still heard to this day, 'you're standing there like Christ Church in Durham Street'.

St Philips or the Drew Memorial, used by the I.R.A. for drilling in the 1940s, was established in 1872 and predated St Mathias's tin church in the Glen Road by some twenty years.

Another tin church, the Luther Memorial, on the mountain lonnan, was consecrated in 1930.

The Methodists had a wee small church in Divis Street. It stood, overshadowed by the huge bulk of Hugh and Dickson's flour mill, at what is now the entrance to Divis Flats. The Presbyterians meanwhile worshipped in Albert Street or up at Broadway. The latter, the Broadway Presbyterian Church, closed due to a dwindling congregation in July 1982. Their church in Albert Street was erected in 1884. The founders of this congregation held their first meeting in 1847 in a hayloft in Conway Street. Five years later they secured the use of a school room in the same street. A church was first erected on the present site in 1854 in what was then a field near Belfast. It was replaced thirty years later by the present church which remained in service until recent times.

Towards the end of the last century, during one of the frequent outbreaks of cholera, priests from St Peter's, some say St Patrick's but I suppose that depends on where you're from, nursed and worked among the Protestant people of the Shankill area. When that area was redeveloped shortly afterwards the residents arranged to have four of the newly built Shankill Road streets named after the Catholic priests who had befriended them, and thus in the heart of loyalist West Belfast we have Blaney Street, Loftus Street, Brennan Street and Meenan Street. This piece of little known history had a happy conclusion recently when some of the old street signs were 'liberated' by a few enterprising priests from St Peter's during the demolition and redevelopment of the Shankill area.

In 1872 the order of nursing nuns, the Bon Secours, was brought by Bishop Dorrian to Belfast and took up residence in Alfred Street. In 1879 the bishop purchased Clonard Lodge on the Falls Road, the residence of W. A. Ross J.P., which was converted into a convent. The nuns attended to the sick of every religious denomination and to the needs of the destitute poor.

In 1885 the increasing size of the Catholic population in the expanding Falls area led to the building of St Paul's Church in Cavendish Street. St Paul's parish took in a lot of the area known as 'up the road', then in the process of expanding around the Broadway Damask Company. From St Paul's to the Donegall Road there were few houses. The lunatic asylum, built in 1829, took in the six acres on which the Royal Victoria Hospital is built and part of it, known locally as the Looney

Pitch or Looney Park was used for football matches or sessions of housey (bingo) by the residents of Leeson Street and the Loney.

The asylum or, to give it its full title, the Belfast District Hospital for the Insane Poor catered for patients from counties Antrim and Down and, for some peculiar reason, the district of Carrickfergus. Getting out may have been a problem but getting in was a job of work in itself, for potential patients not only needed a medical certificate of insanity but also an affidavit of inability to pay for treatment in a private asylum. Highlight of the week for the unfortunate patients, and also no doubt for their neighbours, was the weekly walkabout by inmates, who were preceded on such excursions by a local band.

The doctor in charge of the asylum was a Dr Graham who lived in a large house on the Grosvenor Road near Drew Street. At that time the Grosvenor Road was called Grosvenor Street. It was not until the turn of this century that the doctor and the asylum were moved to Purdysburn. They gave to Belfast the immortal expression, 'you have me ready for Graham's home' often heard in times of tension.

The old asylum always attracted groups of children anxious for a glimpse of the inmates. They, incidentally, were not allowed to smoke and apparently could be seen hanging from the branches of the trees behind the asylum wall begging for cigarettes from passersby.

At that time, on the Falls between the Donegall Road and what is now St James's Road, there were only four newly built houses. Above was Glenalina Terrace, where James Connolly lived, and Clondara Street, Hugo Street and Clondara Terrace. There were few houses between them and Milltown Cemetery. The area between Milltown Row and the cemetery was occupied by St Patrick's Industrial School which moved there from Donegall Street in 1875. The De La Salle Brothers were invited by Bishop MacRory to take charge of it in 1917; and the new director, Brother Joseph Hannigan, purchased twenty-five additional acres of a farm for 'cows and games'. The reformatory section was added later and Fr Flanagan, of Boys' Town U.S.A. fame, was among those to visit the school.

Milltown Cemetery and the City Cemetery were much smaller than they are today. The 'poor ground' in Milltown had been used to bury cholera victims and the City Cemetery had yet to expand into the Glenalina section which was then a muddy swamp known as the Glenalina Dam.

These cemeteries have interesting origins too lengthy to relate here but they were established only after a long haggling match lasting four years between the Catholic Bishop Dorrian and the Belfast Town Improvement Committee of 1866. Plans had been drawn up for a new cemetery to include ten acres for a 'public Roman Catholic ground with a separate entrance and five acres on a site for a Roman Catholic chapel and proprietory Roman Catholic graves; seventeen and a half acres to be allocated as a propietory Protestant ground . . . and the remaining thirteen and a half acres to be allocated as a public grave for all other religious denominations'. The bishop considered that Catholics had not been fairly dealt with and eventually won the concession of a dividing wall between Protestant and Catholic graves plus an extra five acres.

The Privy Council in Dublin met in 1869 to consider the whole affair but by this time Bishop Dorrian had bought a site for a Catholic cemetery at Milltown. He bought it from James Ross at the cost of £4,100.

This new cemetery was consecrated on 18 September 1870 and a congregation of 20,000 people assisted at Mass in a marquee erected on the spot. The City Cemetery opened at around the same time and each cemetery was restricted to its own denomination. Ironically enough today both Catholics and Protestants are buried in the City Cemetery and nobody, least of all the dead, is complaining about it.

The present presbytery of St John's Church was a private residence called Clondara House and Emo Villas, now occupied by Rossa's Gaelic Athletic Club, was the residence of the owners of Grieve's Mills.

The Whiterock area was mainly green fields running right up to the mountain with only a few farms and the red brick terrace near the top of the Whiterock providing human habitation. MacRory Park, now occupied by the British Army, was known as Shaun's Park. It gets its present name from Bishop, later Cardinal, MacRory who presented the park to the Down and Connor diocese causing the Gaelic Athletic Association (G.A.A.) to move to Corrigan Park.

Shaun's Park and the G.A.A. have an interesting early history in Belfast: the first hurling club in the North was the *Tir na nÓg,* which was initially a branch of the Gaelic League and was based at Shaun's Park. This *Tir na nÓg* branch invited

Gas Light

Michael Cusack, founder of the G.A.A., to come to Belfast to set up the association in Ulster. In 1901 they started playing hurling in the Falls Park and then became embroiled in a dispute about whether R.I.C. men were excluded from membership. Shortly after this Bulmer Hobson, who was secretary of the first County Antrim Board of the G.A.A., attempted to develop a junior league, and when the Board showed little interest he resigned and convened a meeting of boys from the Falls Road area. About three hundred attended and it was decided to form a new youth organisation, *Na Fianna Éireann*. Hobson rented Shaun's Park, and Francis Joseph Bigger presented a special trophy for the new junior league. The fledgling Fianna organisation eventually ran into financial difficulties but later, in 1909, Hobson restarted it in Dublin with the help of Countess Markievicz.

During this period the Gaelic League prospered in the Falls area. Indeed, until the mid nineteenth century a number of Gaelic scribes lived in Millfield, transcribing old tracts and manuscripts, and *céilís* were held until recently in halls in King Street, in the *Árd Scoil,* in Sarsfields, in the 'Dal' or Forty-Three Club, and in St Paul's Club. At the turn of the century there were twenty-six branches of the Gaelic League in Belfast, many of them in the Falls area. In 1913 the Belfast Gaelic League supported the families of workers 'locked out' in Dublin.

This cultural awareness was not unique to the Falls area and Belfast has a history of Irish culture going far beyond the famous Harp Festival in 1792 at which Bunting was commissioned to take down the traditional airs played by the assembled harpers. Henry Joy McCracken, his sister Mary Ann, Thomas Russell, 'the man from God knows where', Samuel Neilson and Wolfe Tone were among the audience. Tone, incidentally, was unenthusiastic about the whole affair: he wrote without much relish about the festival in his diary on 11 July and later, on 13 July, he noted 'Harpers again, strum, strum and be hanged'.

A few years later, in 1795, a 'Gaelic Magazine' was launched and in 1835 the Ulster Gaelic Society was established. The vast majority of these early *Gaeilgeorí* were Presbyterians but by the turn of this century ninety-nine percent of the membership of the Gaelic League were Catholics. One P. J. O'Shea, who wrote under the name of *Conán Maol* and taught Irish history to those interested, is remembered not least for describing Elizabeth I as 'that woman with bowels of brass'.

The Catholic hierarchy, trying to cope with their growing congregation in the Falls area, invited the Redemptorists, or 'Redemptists' as they were known locally, to establish a residence in the area. Their first mission in Belfast, and their introduction to Belfast Catholics was in St Mary's in 1872. In subsequent years missions were preached in other city churches until, during a general mission in 1896, Bishop Henry set out to buy Kennedy House, a large two-storied detached building set in fourteen acres of parkland containing a mill dam and bordered by a row of mills. It was approached by a driveway entered through large gates, north of the present O'Neill Street/Odessa Street crossing. The original owners, Victor and James Kennedy, were local businessmen engaged in the spinning of flax and tow.

In 1896 James McConnell purchased the land for building purposes and planned the network of streets which stretch from Dunmore Street to Cupar Street and comprise the present Clonard area. He planned to demolish Kennedy House in order to facilitate the building of a street which would follow and continue the old driveway. Bishop Henry persuaded McConnell to sell him the house and a strip of land around the mill dam — in all three-and-a-half acres — and this alteration caused a change in the proposed direction of the new street, Clonard Gardens, so that it ran between the house and the mill dam. From the day that the first Mass was celebrated on 1 November in Kennedy, by now Clonard, House local people flocked to the new 'chapel', a large room on the ground floor, making their way in the winter mornings and evenings along planks in the muddy avenue between stable lamps which lighted their way.

In 1897, a temporary church with brick walls and a corrugated iron roof was erected and in 1900 when the priests moved to their new monastery and seminary Clonard House became, and still remains, the house for the Sisters of Charity. It was in the 'tin church' in 1897 that the famous 'Clonard Confraternities' of the Holy Family were born. The first superior in Clonard recorded the religious devotion of the people and especially the mill workers in those early days.

> Shortly after the opening of the temporary church I received a letter saying 'Rev. Father, would it be possible to commence the six o'clock Mass five minutes before six? Our signal to commence work goes at six-thirty and we cannot wait for the priest's blessing at the end of Mass and be in time for our work.' Shortly after, I received another letter saying 'Rev. Father, would it be possible to delay the eight o'clock Mass till five after eight? The signal for breakfast in our mill goes at eight o'clock and we could get out to the church and be back to work at nine o'clock.'

In 1911 the present Church of the Holy Redeemer, beside the monastery, was opened and the 'tin church' was demolished, some of the wood and brick being used by the Sisters of Charity to build a wall adjacent to their convent. The remainder was used to raise the level of the monastery gardens while local people took away many pieces of brick and stone as souvenirs.

The religious community in Clonard continues to enjoy a unique relationship, not least for their Clonard Novenas, with the people of the immediate area and with the people of the Falls and greater West Belfast area.

Continued population growth placed increased demands on the Catholic Church. Following the development of Beechmount and Iveagh, St John's was opened as a chapel-of-ease to St Paul's in 1928. The area served by it was sparsely populated at first: four houses in St James's Road and eight in St James's Drive were built as ex-servicemen's houses after the First World War. As a result of the pogroms of the early 'twenties there was a shift of population which saw Catholic refugees squatting in the St James/Rodney complex which was then still being developed and which, indeed, was not completed until the early 'thirties.

Another housing development of the 'twenties was the red-brick estate at Whiterock: rumour (which I refuse to believe as my wife comes from the 'Rock) has it that the first residents were in the habit of keeping coal in their baths. Westrock Bungalows, 'temporary' utility dwellings which are still inhabited, were built between 1939 and 1945 — and Ballymurphy, Glenalina and New Barnsley date from the late 'forties and early 'fifties. Housing in Springhill, Moyard and Springfield Park added, in the 'sixties, still more numbers to the population. St John's had, by 1978 when it was rebuilt, become the church of the largest parish (some 20,000 in number) in the diocese of Down and Connor.

Falls Road Factionalism

Raddy daddy and we're not beat yet
Raddy daddy and we're hardly
Raddy daddy and we're not beat yet
A button for your marley.

Belfast Mill Song

PEOPLE in this part of the world have a benign and protective attitude towards militant republicanism. This is not surprising in a city which conceived the United Irishmen, though the state of enforced limbo in which we live is a more likely reason for such resistance, and those who see the Falls area as a republican stronghold may be surprised to learn that it was not always so.

At the turn of this century the Irish Parliamentary Party was in the ascendant and the republicans were a small, isolated group. The Irish Republican Brotherhood (I.R.B.) in the city was made up mostly of old Fenians who appeared to be more concerned with drinking and reminiscing than with revolution. In 1901 Denis McCullough was sworn into the I.R.B. in Donnelly's public house at Omar Street on the Falls Road. Although initially disenchanted by this introduction to 'the organisation', McCullough commenced to recruit young men into new I.R.B. circles and began a process of getting rid of the older men and tightening up internal discipline. He re-organised the Belfast I.R.B. so effectively that in 1908 he was co-opted to the Supreme Council; he was elected Ulster Representative from 1909 to 1916, becoming President of the Council in December 1915. Born in 1883 and educated by the Christian Brothers, he joined with Bulmer Hobson in forming the Dungannon Clubs, an open debating and literary society which issued a national manifesto in 1905 and grew to a strength of fifty in Belfast, campaigning against recruitment for the British Army and printing many leaflets and postcards which sold widely throughout the country.

Bulmer Hobson was born in Holywood, County Down, and moved to Belfast to a job in a printing works. His family were Quakers and his father a Gladstonian Home Ruler. At the age of twelve he became a subscriber to *An Shan Van Vocht,* a separatist nationalist periodical edited by Alice Milligan and Ethna Carberry with whom he was to become acquainted. In-fluenced by these ladies and by the literary revival of that time, Hobson assisted Maud Gonne MacBride in organising a '98 centenary commemoration which led to the performance of Yeats' *Cathleen Ni Houlihan* in Belfast and the subsequent use of theatre for nationalist propaganda. He joined the Gaelic League and the fledgling Gaelic Athletic Association (G.A.A.) and in 1900 founded the Ulster Debating Society for Boys, an openly non-sectarian and nationalist association which was succeeded by the Protestant National Association whose main aim was to recruit young Protestants for the national move-ment. With David Parkhill, Hobson formed the Ulster Literary Theatre in Clarence Place, which produced plays with an Ulster flavour on political and social conditions. They were joined by such writers as Rutherford Mayne, Lynn Doyle, George Shiel and Harry Morrow of *Thompson in Tír na n'Óg* fame and were successful enough to have Mayne's *The Drone* played in the Opera House.

In 1904 Denis McCullough swore Hobson into the I.R.B. and their combined efforts were directed towards the strengthening of that organisation and towards the politicisa-tion of the citizens of Belfast through the Dungannon Clubs and their newspaper, *The Republic,* which Hobson edited from an of-fice in Royal Avenue. *The Republic* merged six months later with *The Peasant* in Dublin.

In the summer of 1905 Seán Mac Diarmada arrived in Belfast from County Leitrim. Mac Diarmada, later one of the signatories of the 1916 Proclamation, came to Belfast to join his brother Dan who worked in McGlade's Bar. Seán started work as a conductor on the Belfast tramways system and lived in Butler Street in Ardoyne. In those days Belfast, rather than Dublin, was the most populous city in Ireland and many people seeking employment were attracted here from the north-west of the country. The Great Northern and Sligo-Leitrim railways made Leitrim part of the Belfast hinterland, resulting in many Leitrim people being employed in factories and business houses.

MacDiarmada, who came of a republican family, soon became involved with Belfast's republican politics and with the new Sinn Féin association, representing Belfast Sinn Féin at the 1906 convention. In 1907 he became a full-time organiser for the Dungannon Clubs, with a subsidy of thirty shillings a week and a bicycle rented on hire purchase. In April 1907 the Dungannon Clubs and Griffith's *Cumann na nGael* amalgamated as the Sinn Féin League and MacDiarmada was retained as organiser with the Belfast headquarters. By this time he was a member of the I.R.B. and the I.R.B. had begun to organise within Sinn Féin. This was the period during which leading activists, who were to make up the national leadership of the 1916 Rising, were starting to become acquainted with each other. In fact, in 1913 Patrick Pearse was sworn into the I.R.B. by Hobson.

MacDiarmada, McCullough and Hobson all played a major part in the revitalisation of republicanism in Belfast although Hobson later fell out with the other republicans. A lot of their work was done on the Falls Road, with public meetings usually being held after confraternity meetings. Seán Mac-Diarmada probably addressed his first public meeting outside St Paul's Chapel at the Cavendish Street/Falls Road corner when he reluctantly took the place of an absent speaker. Cavendish Street and Cavendish Square, incidentally, were called after Lord Cavendish, the British Secretary-General of Ireland who was killed in Dublin's Phoenix Park by the Invincibles in 1882. For a time, they borrowed a contraption for showing slides from Francis Joseph Bigger and toured the Falls Road's back streets with this novel device, trailing it behind them on a cart, whose owner refused to lend his horse for fear of trouble arising in the area.

Such trouble was expected not from unionist elements but from over-zealous supporters of Joe Devlin, who was elected M.P. for the Falls Division in 1906. There was bitter rivalry between Devlinites and republicans which led in later years to clashes between the groups. Devlin was a leading member of the Irish Parliamentary Party (I.P.P.), a former bar manager in Kelly's Cellars in Bank Lane, and one of the foremost supporters of John Redmond. So popular was he in the Falls area that his was one of the six seats which the I.P.P. managed to retain when that party was routed by Sinn Féin in the 1918 election.

In those early days the Irish Volunteers, the Fianna and the I.R.B. held their meetings in 'The Huts' at Beechmount. 'The Huts' covered an area above and behind where the Broadway Cinema used to stand. They were originally used to billet British soldiers but were later let out as stables for local hawkers and surrounded a grassy area much used for football matches or by women playing 'housey', the illegal forerunner of bingo. During the period when the country was swept by home rule agitation, republicans in the Belfast area had a particularly difficult time. The Ulster Volunteer Force (U.V.F.) had organised against home rule, the I.P.P. was agitating for it and in the wings, waiting to move to the centre of the stage, the republicans were organising. Nora Connolly O'Brien, who lived on the Falls Road during that time, recalls how she remarked to her sister, Agnes:

> 'We're a puzzle to the girls at the works, aren't we? The unionist ones know we are opposed to them and the Ulster Volunteers (U.V.F.) and are nationalists and papishes; and the Catholics know that we don't look upon Redmond as our leader and that we have no love for the Hibs.'

In 1913 more than 4,000 Belfast men joined the Irish Volunteers in the wave of nationalist feeling which swept the country. Later, when Redmond suggested that the Volunteers join the British Army, the Belfast men, influenced by Joe Devlin, did so in such numbers that after the split only 142 men, including Fianna boys, were left under republican control. On Sunday 25 October 1914, Nora Connolly O'Brien was to write the following letter to her father, on the day of a visit by John Redmond to Belfast:

> Dear Daddie,
>
> It's a good thing you were down in Dublin these two days. You would not believe you were living on the Falls Road; you'd think some magician had taken your house and set it down on the Shankill Road. Never were there so many Union Jacks hung out to honour Sir Edward Carson as there were hung out last night and today in honour of J.E. (Redmond). On Friday night I thought it was the limit when I saw the Union Jack on the Catholic Boys Halls along with Belgian flags; great big flags they were, and at the bottom two small threepenny green flags. I was all worked up about it but imagine my feelings when I got a little past Dunville Park on Saturday night to see a monster Union Jack, and alongside it a green banner with the inscription 'Who fears to speak of '98?' . . . One A.O.H. Division had a large Union Jack and a large green flag with a small Union Jack in the corner; underneath, a banner running the entire length of the house, with the inscription: 'We welcome the leader of the National Volunteers to Belfast'. And so it was with every A.O.H. Division. Everywhere along the road was England's flag . . . all the way from King Street to Grosvenor Road.

Fate, however, played a hand and it rained throughout the night so that:

> In the morning their decorations, at least a good few of them, were swirling in the mud and were black with dirt. . . . It rained and poured all morning and never stopped raining all day. The best of it was that they had made no other arrangements, and had to send out word that the meeting was cancelled. There was still the Clonard picture house, where the women and

girls were to present Mrs Redmond with some table linen. Poor woman, I'm sure she needs it. I do not know if any men got in there, but I heard the girls from the mills were there, so there would hardly be room for them. . . .

Despite these conditions, men, women, boys and girls mobilised in Belfast for the 1916 Rising and travelled, as ordered, to Tyrone only to be demobilised and sent back home again, a cause for much bitterness and acrimony afterwards, as no fighting took place in the North.

In 1918, Éamon de Valera was nominated for the Falls Division and was soundly thrashed by Devlin, from whom he seems to have had no chance of winning the seat. The *Irish News* coverage of the election makes interesting reading, for that paper appears to have acted as an election periodical for the Irish Parliamentary Party. Nowhere in its coverage of the election in the Falls Division was one republican statement, speech or election manifesto reported and reporting of republican election activity was minimal. Exposure of Joe Devlin went to the other extreme, and pages were filled with details of his sponsors, expansive reports of his meetings, a parade, election addresses and statements.

De Valera was proposed by D. J. McDevitt of 455 Falls Road and seconded by Denis Maguire of 30 Springfield Road. My Grandfather Hannaway, a prominent full-time union organiser on personal terms with both Larkin and Connolly, worked for de Valera in the election. For his trouble the family home, like others in the area, was placed under siege by Devlinites and attacked by a stone-throwing mob. At one point he and his brother Tommy were fired upon as they returned home after a night's canvassing; and harassment of Sinn Féin workers by Joe Devlin's supporters was continuous and extreme throughout the election campaign. The (London) *Times* carried the following story on 2 December 1918, from their 'own correspondent' in Belfast:

> An attempt by Sinn Féiners yesterday to hold a meeting in the Falls Division of Belfast in support of the candidature of Mr de Valera led to disorderly scenes. A nationalist crowd threw stones and other missiles at the speakers. An at-

tempt was made to capture a Sinn Féin flag and the demonstrators drew truncheons with which they attacked the crowd. The police charged and a number of people including three policemen were injured. Thirteen cases were treated in hospital. Eight arrests were made.

Schools and Scholars

He's off to school wee Hughie
And him not four
Sure I knew the fright was on him
When he left our door
But he took the hand of Dinny
And he took the hand of Dan,
With Joe's oul coat upon him
Ach, the poor wee man.

Elizabeth Shane

DURING the period when the old Loney area was expanding into the Falls district scant attention was paid by the civil authorities to the education of the growing population of young people. While Belfast has a tradition of education going back to the mid eleventh century, the educational system was geared almost exclusively for the rich and illiteracy was rampant among the poor. The national school system was set up in 1830 but included no religious instruction. In 1835 there were only a small number of state schools in Belfast with none at all in the Falls area. Brown Street School in the Shankill catered for five hundred pupils who paid one penny a week for their education; but the lack of facilities for the Catholic poor and the attendance by those Catholic children lucky enough to receive a formal education at Protestant or state schools was a source of frequent controversy. Sunday schools, where a little formal education and a lot of religious instruction was given, were held in various parts of the town and attended reluctantly by some Catholic children.

The first 'ragged school' established in Ireland was in Frederick Street when during the famine year of 1846 the Belfast Ladies Industrial Association set up a national school for girls as 'an independent establishment to preserve a few children from the debasement arising from street begging and waiting for alms at a soup kitchen and although the school is not a lodging it is open to children of the poor who are provided with food, clothing, the three R's and lessons in knitting, sewing and housekeeping'.

On Sunday the children were placed in three categories, the Established Church, Presbyterian and Roman Catholics, and taken to those various churches. Attendance at schools like this fluctuated from seventy to two hundred.

Although there was a ragged school in Barrack Street it served a district of thousands of Catholics. In 1855 an investigation was conducted into the Belfast ladies ragged school following allegations that the school was being used to wean Catholic children away from their own particular religious beliefs and that breakfast was used as a bribe. 'So much stirabout for so much scripture reading.'

To deal with this situation in 1851 the Society of St Vincent de Paul established a Sunday school in St Mary's Chapel Lane which later expanded into the schools of St Mary's Hall. Later, in 1855, they opened a national school in Alexander Street West. Despite their efforts, and those of earlier Catholic schools in Belfast, by 1861 30.2 percent of Belfast Catholics remained illiterate as compared with 10.6 percent of Protestants. The majority of these illiterates lived in the Falls area, and the imbalance was not greatly rectified by the building of a new model school in Divis Street in 1857, at the cost of £14,000.

The situation began slowly to level out when in 1866 the Christian Brothers opened St Mary's School in Divis Street. At that time there were three classrooms with three Brothers in charge and about three hundred and fifty children in attendance. By 1875 a large new classroom was added and one of the former classrooms enlarged so that upwards of seventy extra pupils could attend. In the following year Milford Street School was built. It later became known as St Brendan's and consisted of five classrooms which catered for many children from the

Pound Loney. Conway Street School meanwhile continued to educate both Catholic and Protestant children with an arrangement whereby Catholic children started their day's schooling at 9.00 a.m. with religious instruction, while Protestant children started at 9.30 a.m.

The educational facilities in the Falls area continued their expansion when the Dominican Convent opened in 1870. It was intended that the nuns of the Dominican Order would devote themselves in their large boarding and day schools to the 'educational training of young ladies' in Belfast but as the population of the town was so large national schools were also erected within their grounds. There the nuns gave a 'religious and solid education to girls of the humbler classes' and 'at stated periods, in evening classes to large numbers of the working population'.

In 1880 St Peter's in Raglan Street was opened as was, around the same period, St Paul's Infants in Getty Street and St Patrick's in Balkan Street, while St Joseph's in Slate Street was officially recognised as a national school in April 1883, and in 1900 a school for girls was built in Dunlewey Street. The Sisters of Charity of St Vincent de Paul were invited by the Bishop, Dr Henry, to take charge of it and the school, St Vincent's, catered for five hundred half-timers in four classrooms. The children were taught English, arithmetic, geography, handiwork and music. The first teachers were paid £40 a year by St Peter's parish.

In the same year St Gall's School for Boys opened in Waterville Street with the De La Salle Brothers taking charge. It was intended for the education of 'working boys from St Mary's, St Peter's and St Paul's districts'. Overcrowding at St Gall's necessitated the transfer of the half-timers to another school, St Finian's, which was opened in 1901. This school was housed in part of the Catholic Boys' Hall which was modified for that purpose. In those early days half of the school coal money was paid by St Peter's parish and half by St Paul's. In July 1901 the Brothers moved their residence to 43 Falls Road. They originally lived at 69 Clifton Park Avenue, moving later to 25 College Square North and from there to what is known as the Brother's House just below the library, which incidentally dates from 1908.

At the end of 1924 St Finian's was rebuilt to deal with the influx of new boys following the abolition of the half-timer system (Londonderry Act, 1923). The new school was equipped to accommodate ten teachers and five hundred boys. The Brothers' House also was extended on a plot of land purchased from the Clonard Mill Company and ready for use in 1926. In August 1970 the Brothers made a strategic withdrawal from their front line position at 43 Falls Road to 370 Falls Road and from there to Glenaulin on the Glen Road. Aptly enough, as befitted those times, the building at 43 Falls Road became the headquarters of the Central Citizens' Defence Committee.

The Brothers of St Finian's had the dubious distinction of educating three generations of my family along with numerous other boys from the Falls area. They must also take some of the credit for teaching and encouraging the playing of hurling and Gaelic football in West Belfast, and most of the fine sportsmen who came from the Falls and Loney areas owe their initial contact with these games to the dedication and patience of such teachers.

One famous old-timer was Brother Benignus, called the Bore because of his shouted encouragement to 'bore in lads, bore in'. Until his death in retirement, not so many years ago, he could be seen taking his daily walk along the Falls Road. Another old timer, Brother Charles, for years exhausted our patience with his gentle efforts to form a school choir, a penance he undertook with subsequent rewards at *feiseanna,* through generations of tone-deaf scholars. Johnny Blake, a small, tweedy, pipe-smoking gentleman, was another stalwart of St Finian's.

Young teachers like Mr Nolan, Brother Christopher and Brother Aloysius did their best with us and, scholastic enterprises to one side, unruly mobs of young boys armed with hurling sticks first learned the pleasures of the camogie pitch in the Falls Park, through the dedication of these young men. I often wonder where these teachers, alive or dead, are now, and I am sure that many others who enjoyed their kindness as well as the sting of slaps from their straps are equally curious.

> Our school's a nice wee school
> Made of bricks and plaster
> The only thing that we don't like
> Is our wee baldy master,
> He goes to the pub on Saturday night
> He goes to Mass on Sunday

To pray to God to give him strength
To slaughter us on Monday.

Some of these old schools of the Falls area have vanished now, of course. Conway Street was burned out in a pogrom on 11 July 1936, forcing the transfer of its 'refugee' teachers and pupils to St Brendan's in Milford Street. St Comgall's, one of the more recent schools, was built in 1932 on the site of the old model school which was destroyed in the 'twenties and the ruins, populated by roosting pigeons, remained desolate until local people succeeded in raising the money required to erect the new St Comgall's. St Brendan's, which had been closed as a condemned building when St Comgall's was opened, had to be re-opened to deal with the influx of pupils and teaching staff from Conway Street. St Brendan's was finally demolished in 1967 to make way for Divis Flats and as redevelopment continued Getty Street and its school were to meet the same fate.

Fortunately, most of the schools on the front of the road remain and if you pass St Finian's today you will see scores of noisy boys playing football in the school yard, as they have for decades; being shepherded towards the gate by Ruby, the caretaker around whom the whole school revolves; or being patiently observed by Brother Declan, the present school principal, who has an uncanny talent of knowing every pupil by name. With the number of changes on the Falls Road in recent years St Finian's appears to be one of the few institutions to remain unaltered and unmarked by demolition, war or British government cuts. Long may it continue.

Dèja Vu

For this Edward Fitzgerald died,
And Robert Emmet and Wolfe Tone
All that delirium of the brave?

W. B. Yeats

THE old man drew heavily on his Park Drive and settled back on the settee.

'So you want to know about the 'twenties', he declared, gazing past potted geraniums through lace curtains at the grey half-demolished street. It was a Thursday evening. He was due to shift on Monday. 'They wanted me to go on Saturday but I told them I'd go in my own good time. A Saturday flit is a short sit. So I'm going on Monday. My next stop after that will be Milltown. There's not many of us left, you know. I was born here. Thought I'd be buried from here as well.'

He sighed and reflected in silence. Then, decided, he deftly poked the dying fire into life, flicked the Park Drive butt into the newly born flames and handed me a battered photograph album.

'That's me and my mates. We worked just around the

corner from here in the stables. There was stables all around here, you know. Nearly any wee court or yard you see was a stable. I recall a herd of cows in the ones in Leeson Street and pigs round in Cyprus Street. A lot of people kept chickens as well. That's Jimmy there: he worked for a street hawker, kept his horse in Balaclava Street; I was in Sevastopol Street, cleaned the stables night and morning; and that's Paddy', a stubby finger identified Paddy. 'I haven't seen Jimmy since Paddy's funeral. He's up in Twinbrook now with his daughter; says he'd rather be down the road. Paddy minded the horses in Ross Street and then he worked in Kinahan's. That's our Seán. He went to the States. He wouldn't know the place now if he came back. You know, when me, Jimmy, Paddy and Seán were wee bucks the Falls was a great place. People nowadays don't know they're living. We had our troubles, same as today, but the neighbours were good. We looked after our own, be they sick or old, drunk or sober. No need for meals on wheels in them days.'

He thumbed through faded photographs, stopping only to light another cigarette. 'I used to know your grandfather, you know. He was the first of the Adams's to turn republican. Him and the Elliots and the Begleys — Paddy Begley, your granny's brother, was a handy boxer. Fought under the name of Boyd. That's why everybody called him Boyd Begley. Though you wouldn't recall that. I remember him fighting Kenny Webb, the Irish champion.

'That's my mother there. She reared nine of us in this house. I'm the only one left. She always told me she wouldn't be happy till I was married and settled. Well, I settled okay,' he smiled, 'but I never did get round to marrying. Ach, we had good times then. There was big stones, you know, outside every door and on summer nights the women would sit outside their doors and play housey. The streets were cobbled then; no motor cars. The coalman — we bought coal by the stone — the milkman, hawkers and the like all had horses and carts. The milkman ladled out the milk into jugs with a big measure. Many a time I got a jug of milk and a pitcher of buttermilk. Real buttermilk with dollops of cream and butter floating on top.

'All the womenfolk baked: like, we got a ticket of shop bread or a Barney Hughes bap every so often, but mostly me ma baked on the griddle. Treacle farls and soda farls, and bannocks or wheaten and potato bread. Potato apple or bread puddings would be a special treat. I'm making myself hungry with

all this talk of food! Go on in there like a good man and stick us
on a cup of tea. You'll find bread in the cupboard. And don't
mind the mess: this place is like Maggie Marley's with me shifting. I couldn't be annoyed doing anything with it. Sure,
what's the point?'

He fell silent again as I rummaged in the tiny scullery,
rinsing cups in the jawbox — the big stone sink — and wetting
the tea.

'You know,' he shouted in to me, 'there was none of
these so-called modern amentities in those days. No wirelesses,
well very few anyway, only crystal sets in the beginning and all
of them tuned in, round here anyway, to Radio Eireann. And
no TV's. TV is a curse. We made our own fun. No, things were
simpler then. See this?'

I returned with tea and a plate of bread and butter.

'See this?' he pointed to the coffee table. 'Well, we had a
white scrubbed table and four scrubbed chairs. Me da had an
armchair, the only one in the house: it sat here, where I am
now, at the fire. All the houses had ranges and a gas ring on the
hob. No electric lights: two gas mantles; we used candles up the
stairs and in the scullery. A cupboard for food and sometimes
bits of clothing and that was that. Big double beds upstairs and
in the back room. We slept head to foot, five in the back and two
in the front with me ma and da. Our Kathleen and Ena slept
down the street in their granny's. There was a gas lamp outside
the front door — you can still see the mark — they tuk it down a
couple of years ago. Used to be able to read by it. And the floors
were tiled: great fuss here with the mother and sisters every
week, scrubbing the tiles and the furniture, doing the brasses
and black-leading the grate. But I suppose you don't want to
hear all this. You'd think my head was cut the way I'm going
on. No visitors, you see. Though I read a lot. What was it exact-
ly you wanted to hear about?'

He gazed at me, supping his tea and chewing one of the
pieces of bread.

'You want to know about the troubles in the 'twenties?
Ah, now,' he chuckled, 'I hope you've plenty of time for listen-
ing. There's many a story I cud tell: make your teeth curl, but,'
he paused mischievously, 'you never know who you're talking
to. Can't be too careful nowadays.' Then, laughing at my
discomfort, 'I'm only having you on. To tell you the truth, I
consider myself a bit of a historian. Once I get my thoughts in

order I'll give you your fill of facts and figures. You're in no rush you said? Well, you know that the United Irishmen was founded in Belfast, in Sugar House Entry? All sorts of famous people came to Belfast. John Mitchel, Daniel O'Connell, Thomas Francis Meagher, Michael Davitt. I used to read about them all. Henry Joy, Russell — he's "the man from God knows where" — Jemmy Hope, Orr, Harry Munro and the rest of them used to meet in Sugar House Entry. Henry Joy's family, the McCrackens, owned some of the cotton and linen mills in Belfast. He was hanged in Corn Market. Was interned for a while in Dublin, if my memory serves me right. They were all hanged in the end or deported. Mostly Presbyterians. Funny how people change. Things never change, you know, only people.'

He poked at the fire again, then satisfied with the result settled back and continued. 'Anyway, when I was a young fellah, we had our troubles as well, not as bad as nowadays but rough enough just the same. I recall my mother talking about the Fenians, sitting here at night at this very hearth. Some of them's commemorated in the monument in Milltown, at the old Republican plot. Now wait till we see: there's William Harbinson, a great man altogether. He was a colour-sergeant in the Antrim Militia stationed in the barracks in North Queen Street. The Fenians infiltrated the British Army, you know. No chance of that nowadays. Anyway, Harbinson died in Belfast Prison; he was only forty-four. Buried up in County Antrim, I think in Ballinderry. The first monument in Milltown was erected in his memory; it was blew up in 1937. It also commemorated about seventy other ones including over twenty Protestant Fenians — that's a contradiction, people would say nowadays: ignorance is a great man — and some Yanks who came over as part of an expeditionary force from the States. They ended up in Belfast Prison as well. Does a great trade does "the Crum". It was built in 1846 you know.'

He lit another cigarette. 'I remember, in 1919, with all the talk of home rule, that there was a great strike for a forty-four hour week. The gas department and the electricity — that didn't affect us — the trams were laid up and the bakeries, even the mills were idle. We used to sing "We'll work no more till we get the forty-four, on the good ship *Lullabell*". Then Carson started to rouse up the Orangemen. This state was born in trouble and has caused trouble ever since.

Divis

'Did you ever hear of Ned Trodden? Well, Ned had a barber's shop on the Falls: number 68. He was prominent in the I.R.B. and in the 'twenties Sinn Féin and the I.R.A. held meetings in Ned's shop. One night towards the end of 1920, two peelers were shot dead up the road at Broadway. The Specials used the Beehive Bar as a billet in them days. Anyway, in the early hours of the morning Ned's door knocked and when Ned called out "Who's that?" he received the reply "Military to raid". Now, then like now, that wasn't an unusual occurrence so young Eddie, the son, went down and opened the door and outside what do you think but weren't there four men with their faces all blackened and rifles in their hands. Eddie tried to slam the door but they forced their way in and fired a shot at him as he charged up the stairs. Then they poured petrol all over the kitchen and threatened to burn the family out. Eventually, they made their way up and took Ned down and into the backyard where they shot him dead. They also broke his arms in two places. They murdered two other men the same way that night. Sean Gaynor, he was a volunteer as well, played for O'Connell's hurling club, and Seán McFadden. The two of them lived on the Springfield Road. It was the peelers done it. Volunteer Don Duffin and his brother Pat from Clonard Gardens suffered the same fate. It wasn't long after that, and I wasn't long left school, that I became connected. I remember well the day they were buried. We hardly went over the door that week. With reprisals and the like, people were cowed to some extent, afraid of the knock on the door, waiting for the "B" men or the peelers to call. An old invalid man was shot dead like that in Varna Street. Of course, the I.R.A. did a good deal of shooting as well but they were so outnumbered and partition had cut off the nationalists so much that the I.R.A. spent most of its time defending areas or trying to reassure people.'

He paused for a minute unravelling a piece of fluff from a cushion beside him. Then with a smile he said, 'The ambush in Raglan Street was an exception, of course. A cage-car was lured into Raglan Street and ambushed. I don't recall it clearly myself; just heard the shooting and then the talk around the area. You know I couldn't even tell you what casualties, if any, there were. My head's away. I do remember long afterwards that Hughie McMenamy, he was in charge of issuing Free State pensions, he told me that if all those who applied for a pension because they were involved in the Raglan Street ambush had really been there then they could have ate up the cage-car, peelers and all.

'All the areas had to have stand-bys, against the Orangemen, especially in places like Ballymacarrett. That wee district came under attack a good few times. I recall the funeral of an I.R.A. volunteer, Murtagh McAstocker. He was shot dead during the pogroms and his funeral was massive. The British military drove armoured cars through the ranks of marching mourners to try to break up the funeral cortège. They didn't succeed, though. There was an I.R.A. firing party at the graveside and shots were fired over the grave at Milltown. We used to lie all night around Clonard Chapel on stand-by against the Orangemen just like at the start of these troubles.

'There were men from here fought in the South as well, you know. Seán O'Carroll lived in Gibson Street: his family came originally from Celbridge in Kildare and as he grew up here he became invoved with the volunteers. He became O.C. of "D" Company. A great man with the Irish language. He went to Ardee to teach the language there and he was shot dead in a reprisal shooting by the Black and Tans. He's buried in Milltown and in Ardee they've a street named after him. And then there was Seán MacCartney from Norfolk Street. He was on active service with a Belfast flying column in County Cavan. He was shot dead in the Lappinduff mountains during a fierce engagement with the British Army.'

Outside, the rain threw itself in handfuls against the window, forcing our attention to the grey sky beyond our warm room. The old man was undeterred. 'Don't you know that Joe McKelvey was from Cyprus Street, just around the corner from here. Joe's da was a sergeant in the R.I.C. and the family came to live here when the da was stationed at Springfield Road. When the da died Joe became active in the Fianna and then in the I.R.A., eventually becoming O.C. of the 3rd Northern Division. After the split over the treaty in 1921 he was appointed Assistant Chief of Staff to Liam Lynch, and for a time he acted as Chief of Staff. He was arrested in the Four Courts when the English lent the Free Staters the guns to attack the I.R.A. garrison there. And well you know what happened then. Rory, Liam, Dick and Joe were shot dead by the Staters in the prison yard of Mountjoy, without charge or trial on the Feast of the Immaculate Conception, 1922. We brought Joe's

body home two years later. The four men executed were from
each province of Ireland. That was a black day in Irish history;
and not too long ago either. Then things started to settle a bit
after the Civil War; on the surface at least. There were men in
jail for years after, interned and sentenced, and great poverty
everywhere. The curfews that went on for about four-and-a-
half years were lifted in 1924. We were beaten but not defeated
and they knew it, so they gave no quarter, and man, woman
and child from the areas lived as displaced persons, oppressed
by the Northern government and deserted by Dublin. And
that, son,' he looked at me for a long quiet minute, 'was the
'twenties. Nowadays, the crowd in Dublin think Ireland stops
at Dundalk. Whatever freedom they have, and I don't think it's
that much the way they kow-tow to Thatcher, they would
have less if it wasn't for the people of the North.' He smiled
weakly. 'The North began, the North held on, God bless the
Northern land.'

'What about the 'thirties and 'forties?' I asked.

'The 'thirties and the 'forties? You come round to see
me in my new house and I'll tell you about them times. We've
stirred up too many memories today for an oul man. Not that I
didn't enjoy my life. I've had a long innings and I regret none of
it. But I'm not used to talking so much. Come round next
Wednesday. You've got my address, haven't you? Well, I'll be
settled in then and I'll dig out some oul papers for you. Okay?
You'll see yourself out? Thinking of shifting out of this oul
house has me near destroyed. G'wan on now *a mhic* and don't
be heeding an oul man's gurnings.'

I left him in his chair by the fire and pulled the front door
after me. His was the last house left occupied in the street. I
rapped the window at him on my way past and he grinned at me
and waved a cheery goodbye.

That's the way the removal men found him on Monday,
sitting in his chair by a dead fire, gazing with lifeless eyes past
potted geraniums through lace curtains at the grey half-
demolished street he was born in.

The 'Thirties and the 'Forties

A toiling and a moiling
Oh what a life of bliss
They'll promise you heaven in the next life
While they're robbing you in this.

                                    from *Strumpet City*

THE 'thirties opened with the Outdoor Relief riots and closed with internment, prison ships, mass unemployment, and a world war.

The system of paying social security to those who were unemployed and on the starvation line was known as Outdoor Relief, and it was administered by the unionist-dominated 'Poor Law Guardians'. They, in the face of unemployment mounting to 100,000 in the Six Counties, refused to make payments to the increasing numbers of long-term unemployed.

On 3 October 1932, 600 Outdoor Relief men went on strike. They were supported and organised by the Unemployed Workers' Movement and by the Revolutionary Workers' Group, and had five demands:

> (1)   Abolition of task work (i.e. labour test to

qualify for relief).

(2) Increase in scale of relief to a man of 15s. 5d. per week, wife 8s. 3d. per week, each child 2s.

(3) No payment in kind — all relief to be paid in cash.

(4) Street improvement work under Exceptional Distress Relief Scheme, or scheme of like character, to be done at trade union rate of wages.

(5) Adequate outdoor allowance to all single unemployed men and women who were not in receipt of unemployment benefit.

Within a few days thousands of Belfast workers, Protestant and Catholic, were on the march in support of these demands. The unionist régime reacted in a time-honoured and predictable manner: they banned the marches and proceeded to try to divide the workers. My Uncle Paddy has a vivid recollection of what happened then.

'The people without work, supported and organised by the republicans and other elements, resisted the government and its bans. I recall a whole crowd of us getting together down our way. We were not as well organised as the kids are today. But at that time we were all together, all united: the Shankill, the Falls and Sandy Row, everyone united. They all marched up to the Union. About ten thousand marched up and demanded admittance. According to the law they couldn't refuse them. Of course, ten thousand couldn't get in but the gesture was there. Some of them got in. Peter Shannon spent the night in it.

'That was the best time the Protestants and Catholics ever came together, that particular time. United we were and the only way they could divide us was to shoot a couple of Catholics. They shot John Geehan down in Leeson Street. They shot him dead. I remember it well. They shot another Catholic dead as well and wounded many others.

'I recall at that time the peelers used to charge down Leeson Street and we used to counter-charge them. We were only a crowd of young lads. Well, one time we charged up towards them. They were gathered about the third house from the top and when we got as far as Cairns Street they opened fire.

I remember very clearly a certain sergeant from Springfield Road Barracks taking aim. We scattered, naturally enough. Down Getty Street, Abercorn Street and Cairns Street. There was a wee fellah shot at the corner of Abercorn Street. Me and John Garland ran out and dragged him down to McMullan's house. He was shot in the spine. I remember lifting his shirt and seeing the bullet hole in his back. We dashed off to the Royal and got an ambulance. I went with him to the Mater. I remember saying "God help him" while the peelers taunted us in the ambulance.

'We took up the tar blocks and dug pits across the streets to prevent the cage-cars coming into the area. I remember one cage-car opening up and wounding oul Dough Brady. She was a local character and she was up in Panton Street. She was shot in the shoulder and oul Jimmy Doherty, another character, was carrying her over to the hospital. She wasn't worried about the wound in her shoulder but about the way Jimmy was carrying her.

'"Jesus, Jimmy," she was shouting. "Ah Jesus, Jimmy, mind my clothes, keep my clothes down." That caused a great laugh around the district afterwards.

'Anyway, they shot the Catholics and waved the Union Jack and as far as unity between the Catholics and Protestants was concerned that was the rioting over. We won the demands but the unity, unfortunately, was shortlived.'

Frightened by the threat that united working class agitation presented to their interests, the government announced new terms for the payment of the unemployed. At a mass meeting in St Mary's Hall, these terms were voted on and accepted. The following day tens of thousands of people marched in the funeral cortège of Samuel Baxter, one of those shot in the riots, up the Falls Road to Milltown Cemetery. On 17 October the workers returned to work and slowly, if uneasily, things returned to normal, or to what passes for normality in this part of the world.

Several significant developments arose from the strike. On the one hand, the unionists organised the Ulster Protestant League in order to prevent any further coming together of Protestant and Catholic workers. On 15 October the newly formed League announced:

We deplore that those unfortunate conditions

were used as a cloak by the Communist Sinn
Féin element to attempt to start a revolution in
our province. We also greatly deplore that
some of our loyal Protestant unemployed were
misled to such an extent that they associated
themselves with enemies of their faith and principles.

On the other hand, the radical tendency within the
I.R.A., encouraged by the experience in Belfast, continued to
play a part in social and labour agitations. In support of the
railway strike in the Six Counties they blew up bridges and
railway property and attacked blacklegs as well as engaging in
more passive solidarity actions.

These and similar developments in other parts of
Ireland led to the short-lived Republican Congress and to the
presence of three bus-loads of Shankill Road workers at the
annual Republican Wolfe Tone Commemoration at
Bodenstown in 1934. Unfortunately a minority element at the
ceremony were less than delighted by their attendance and by
their banner, which read 'Break the connection with
capitalism' and a disgraceful fracas broke out. And this during
a time when, to quote my Uncle Paddy again, 'Feudalism and
"yes sir, no sir" was the working régime which people had to
accept. When I worked in Kinahan's we didn't address
Kinahan as Mr Kinahan. He had to be addressed as Mr
Henry. Workers had to accept that their employers expected
them to grovel.'

Against this background, life went on as usual in the
Falls. The hungry 'thirties are remembered, with irony, in this
song of those times:

Bacon Cuttings
Now the boys around here
Drink stout and beer
Blowhard and tawny wine
And when they're drinking tawny
Sure they think they're doing fine
But I don't go for stuff like that
For I'm not such a glutton
Because the only thing that I like best
Is a pound of bacon cuttings.

Chorus
Cuttings, cuttings, I love bacon cuttings
Ham and eggs may do their best
For other kinds of gluttons
But I go down to Gresham Street
And into Lizzie Huttons
And I throw my cap along the floor
And I shout for bacon cuttings.

Now the last time I was arrested
Sir James Craig paid my fine
He dressed me up in an evening suit
And sat me down to dine.
The waiter, he came up to me
'Is yours a steak or mutton?'
'Ach' says I 'get away out o' that
Sure mine's a bacon cutting.'

Chorus

A football league for the unemployed was organised locally. The Liam Mellowes team was made up of players from around Abercorn Street and Raglan Street while the Kevin Barry drew its team from below Varna Street opening. They helped to keep Gaelic football alive, while soccer players from that part of the area made up the Seaforth team. Handball leagues flourished also, with great rivalry between different streets and well supported matches at Raglan Street and other street corners throughout the area.

Walks to Charlie Watters' pub at Hannahstown were a regular pastime for local people. Later, in the 'fifties these walks were organised for a short period as an annual sporting event but in the 'forties they were more a form of recreation enjoyed by all Falls Road people, young and old, male and female.

In 1942 Gerard O'Callaghan, a nineteen-year-old I.R.A. man from Cavendish Street was shot dead not far from Watters', at Budore, by an R.U.C. raiding party. The Stormont government refused to allow an inquest to be held. Shortly before this, two other Falls Road volunteers, Joe Malone from Cullingtree Road and Terence Perry from Ton Street, died in Parkhurst Prison. Republican funerals were once again going up the Falls Road to Milltown Cemetery. My father narrowly missed one when he was shot and seriously injured by the R.U.C. in Leeson Street. Earlier, in 1940, the Catholic Bishop, Dr Mageean, had walked behind the coffin of Jack Gaffney who had been interned on Christmas Eve 1938 and had died on the prison ship *Al Rawdah* on 18 November 1940.

In 1942 Tom Williams from Bombay Street was hanged in Belfast Prison. His remains still lie buried there. He had been wounded and captured in Cawnpore Street following a shooting incident at the corner of Kashmir Road and Clonard Gardens. During his arrest an R.U.C. man was shot dead. Tom and five men captured with him were sentenced to hang but because of the public outcray a last minute reprieve was granted to five of them. Tom Williams was hanged on 2 September; he was nineteen years old. Another who died then was Rocky Burns, killed in a shoot-out with the R.U.C. in Queen Street.

During this period the Falls area was a hotbed of Republican activity. Charlie McGlade, a native of the Bone area, recalls a system of safe houses around Baker Street, Bow Street and Massareene Street and recounts how he and Seán McCaughey, who was later to die on hunger-and-thirst strike while 'on the blanket' in Portlaoise Prison, used to clamber across yard walls and down entries to escape R.U.C. raiding parties.

Harrassment by the R.U.C. continued. This song of an earlier time shows that such messing about was nothing new, especially for such unfortunates as poor Maggie Walsh:

> I'm a decent wee girl, Maggie Walsh is my name
> I was born in the Loney, the Falls Road, the same
> Sure I went over by Millfield and the peelers were
> there
> They put their hand on my shoulder and then called
> a car.
> It was early next morning about ten o'clock
> Before Judge McCarthy I was placed in the dock
> He put on his eyeglass and to me he did say
> 'Is it you Maggie Walsh, that's before me this day?
> If it had been your first time sure you might have
> gone free
> But this is your third time on the book, I can see

One month, I'll give you, you'll be out off the way
For shouting "Home Rule" on St Patrick's Day!'
Sure the warder comes in and he opens your cell
'Roll up your oul blankets and empty your poe
And right about turn to the bone yard you go.'

The prisons were full, repression severe and German bombers flew overhead driving people to sleep in the air-raid shelters which dotted the streets or in the fields below the mountain. But still despite it all, and perhaps in many ways because of it all, life in the Falls continued against a background of unemployment, emigration, raids, shooting incidents and arrests. It was not until the late 'forties that the people here could settle down into the periodic peacefulness that broke out every decade. The world war with its Yankee soldiers, German bombs, blitz and ration books was to usher in an era of change. Nothing really substantial, more a change in attitudes, with the 'yes sir, no sir' syndrome dying a slow death and the welfare state with its almost equal educational opportunities forcing itself upon a reluctant unionist government. And it was ironic in the light of all their sectarianism and loyalty, and all the republican subversion, that a man called McGuinness from the Falls won the Victoria Cross, symbolising to some degree that such valour, if misguided, was non-sectarian, at least until the recipient and his fellow soldiers returned home again. Because nothing had really changed. After the shouting had died down, Stormont continued to be 'a Protestant parliament for a Protestant people.' As James Craig declared, 'All I boast is that we are a Protestant parliament and a Protestant state.'

In fact Sir Basil Brooke, who was to become the third prime minister of Stormont summed up, in the early 'thirties, the view of the unionist ruling class, then and now, when he condemned 'Protestants and Orangemen who employ Roman Catholics. I feel I can speak freely on this subject as I have not a Roman Catholic about my place. I recommend those people who are loyalists not to employ Roman Catholics, ninety-five percent of whom are disloyal.'

My Aunt Jane

My Aunt Jane has a bell on the door
A white stone step and a clean swept floor
Candy apples, hard green pears
Conversation lozenges.

Belfast Street Song

OUR street gang used to wage war on a regular basis with the crowd from Getty Street, based mostly on the old theme of cowboys and Indians, cops and gangsters or Germans and Americans. The British were rarely involved in our war games though we all read the usual English comics. It was all good sport, rarely becoming a real fight: more a case of charge and counter-charge, like the siege of Limerick. On the few occasions when things got serious real warfare was averted by the verbal byplay which usually guaranteed adult intervention and a temporary cessation of hostilities.

'I'll knock your wine in.'

'You and whose army? You cudn't knock anybody's wine in. G'wan home or you'll get a dig in the bake.'

'Com'n up here and say that. You're only good for mouthing and slabbering, you think you're a big man. The only thing big about you is your mouth.'

'You're luking your melt kicked in, wee buck. I'll make you slobber on the other side of your gub if you come up here. You're yellah. You cudn't beat the deck.'

A favourite preliminary to a real scrap, usually between individuals in Getty Street Entry, was an assertion that this was 'in earnest'. On occasions the combatants, irked by some insult, were likely to be from the same gang.

'You watch your mouth, your're ganching there.'

'Who do you think you're talking to? You're getting on my wick, you're looking your head in your hands. Do you want a fair dig?'

'Fair dig? You wudn't know a fair dig if it hit you in the face. I'm in earnest. If you don't lay off I'll take my temper out on you.'

If both parties proceeded to 'take their tempers out', the rest of us formed a ring and refereed collectively with loud assertions that this was a 'fair dig'.

'Everybody else keep out of it.'

'No scrabbing and no putting the boot in.'

Sometimes things got difficult if bigger brothers were about. They tended to accept fair digs only while their relatives weren't getting a hiding. Then they joined the fray with a shouted excuse of 'I saw that. You took a Judas on him. C'mon and try somebody your own size.' Or, 'I'm not letting you away with that, you sleekit wee get. I'll teach you to pull hair. You fight like an oul doll.'

When things got really serious, which was a rare occurrence, passing adults or neighbours signalled their disapproval with much bellowing and shouting.

'G'wan away out o' that you wee skitters. Kicking up a racket there! Why don't you fight outside your own doors, disgracing yourselves rolling in the muck like that. Wait till I see your mothers. Don't be standing there gaping at me like that, ya cheeky imps, I'll put my toe up your arse, g'wan take yourselves away off to your own street.'

A rush and we were off, shouting and yelling before such an Amazonian onslaught. Male interruptions were much more tedious. They tended to intervene physically, trailing combatants apart and lecturing them on the merits of a fair dig as opposed to merely wrestling on the ground. Usually this happened only when the wee bucks 'keeping dick' were surprised and delayed in shouting 'Watch it lads, skeedaddle!'

Despite such occasional outbursts, there was normally a state of peaceful coexistence between ourselves and our elders, and handball or softball soccer matches were always suspended when womenfolk passed.

'Hould the ball there. Let Missus Johnson by. Watch that wee kid.'

Handball was played at Harbinson's gable or down at the junction of Abercorn Street, Dunville Street and Sorella Street. Soccer matches dashed up and down between lamp posts on opposite sides of the pavement and shootieins, penalties or rushies were conducted down at the rag store. These games, weather permitting, were played throughout the year.

In the summer we made guiders or had them made for us, pressing pram wheels and planks into service for the mad rush down Dunville Street. Ball-bearings were much in demand. Short-planked guiders, big wheels to the front with a single or double ball-bearing at the rear ensured a real weeker of a guider. We also had a hoop and cleek season, the hoop improvised from the spokeless rim of an old bicycle wheel, the cleek made from bull wire, looped to make a handle at one end with a U-shaped cleek by which the hoop was guided at the other. The real test of skill was in one's ability to make the hoop reverse its flight and come back to its owner.

Our elders must have had infinite patience because the small back streets reverberated to the hum of ball-bearing guiders and the clatter of hoops for the few months that these noisy playthings remained in season. Mossycock, cribby, kick-the-tin, and rally-oh were less noisy games. We also played rounders with a hurling stick, until the Christian Brothers taught us the merits and skills of hurling itself. Marbles, or marleys, was perhaps the most regularised of our past-times. For some reason unknown even yet to me, all of a sudden everybody seemed to know that it was marley season. In the summer time old men played it in a little marley-pitch in the Dunville Park but we played it everywhere, along the pavements and on the street itself. There were bewlers and dinkies, shooters and ballies. The bewlers were large 'knuckle busters', dinkies were small highly prized miniatures; shooters, favourite scarred and proven score getters; and ballies were the sometimes illegal ball bearings. There were various ways of playing marleys. In one, the object was to knock your opponent or opponent's man out of the chalked circle; in another, to hit him from a measured distance; and in yet another, to succeed in dribbling into a hole in the ground. Some boys were expert at bunking, others at dribbling, most at spanning. Ricochets were often disputed but cheating was difficult and as most games were evenly contested, being completely 'cleaned out' was a rare occurrence. When wet days prevented outdoor sessions we played an indoor game by cutting holes in the base of a shoe or sweetie box and endeavoured to shoot directly into them.

We rarely mixed with wee girls, who minded their own business even when we interrupted their games of hop-scotch; one, two, three red lights, swings, queenie-oh or skips. They played house with dolls, sometimes dressing up and chalking out a kitchen which stretched from the front hall out into the pavement. They also played 'two balls' or 'three balls' against a wall much more expertly than any of us could have, though we would not have admitted it in those days. Anyway, for any boy to have been caught competing would have made for much slagging and reddeners all round.

Swings, simply made by looping rope and tightening it around a lamp post, were particularly favoured by girls. They also played with spinning tops or peeries, a game which we enjoyed as well. In the summer days both sexes converged in separate groups upon Dunville Park where swings, see-saws, slides and a witch's hat were much abused. Playing in the bushes with the added thrill of a chase by the wackey was strictly a boys' province, as were cheesers which we collected from the chestnut trees at the Falls Park.

The girls I recall, always seemed to sing a lot.

> Five o'clock is striking
> Mother may I go out
> My true love is awaiting
> For me without.
> First he bought me apples
> Then he bought me pears
> And then he gave me sixpence
> To kiss him on the stairs.
>
> I wouldn't take his apples
> I wouldn't take his pears

And I gave him back his sixpence
When he kissed me on the stairs.

Queenie-oh, Queenie-oh, who's got the ball?
I haven't got it in my pocket.

A bhalla, Mrs Brown, a bhalla Mrs Brown,
A bhalla, bhalla, bhalla, bhalla, bhalla, Mrs
Brown.
A stampie, Mrs Brown, a stampie Mrs Brown,
A stampie, stampie, stampie, stampie, stampie Mrs
Brown.
A dashie Mrs Brown, a dashie Mrs Brown,
A dashie, dashie, dashie, dashie, dashie, Mrs
Brown.

The wind, the wind, the wind blew high,
The rain came tumbling from the sky.
Oul..........says she'll die,
If she doesn't get the fellah with the roving eye.
She is handsome, she is pretty,
She is the belle of Belfast city,
She is courting, one, two, three,
Please won't you tell me who is she.

Lady, lady, tip the ground,
Lady, lady, give a bourl round,
Lady, lady, show your shoe,
Lady, lady, run right through.

When I was sick and very very sick
And in my bed I lay,
The only thing that cured my head,
Was to see the green flag flying.
The green, the green, the lovely, lovely green,
The green that shall be worn,
But the orange, the orange, the dirty, dirty orange,
The orange shall be torn.

One, two, three O'Leary,
I spy de Valeary,

Sitting on his bumboleary,
Eating sugar candy.

De Valeary had a canary
Up the leg of his drawers.
When he was sleeping
It was peeping
Up the leg of his drawers.

King Billy had a cat,
It sat upon the fender,
And every time it saw a rat,
It shouted 'No surrender'.

My Aunt Jane she called me in,
She gave me tea out of her wee tin,
Half a bap and sugar on the top,
And three wee lumps out of her wee shop.

My Aunt Jane she's terrible smart,
She bakes wee cakes and apple tarts,
And when Halloween comes around
Fornenst a tart I'm always found.

There was a wee man and we called him Dan,
He washed his face in the frying pan,
He combed his hair with a donkey's tail,
And scratched his belly with his big toe nail.

A rosy apple, a lemon and a pear,
A bunch of roses she shall wear,
A golden bracelet by her side,
And she'll take.......to be her bride.

He takes her down the lily white shore,
He takes her over the water,
He gives her kisses three or four,
For she is the miller's daughter.

I've a boy from America,
And another one at sea, at sea,

The shop at the top of Leeson Street.

And another in Australia,
That's the one who'll marry me, marry me.

First he took me to the pictures,
Then he took me to the ball, to the ball,
Then he ran away and left me,
That's the one who did it all, it all.

Over the garden wall
I let the baby fall
My mammy came out
And gave me a clout
I asked her what
She was talking about
She gave me another
To match the other
Over the garden wall.

I'm a little teapot, small and stout
Here's my handle, here's my spout
When the kettle's boiling hear me shout
'Tip me up and pour me out'.

In and out go dusty bluebells
In and out go dusty bluebells
In and out go dusty bluebells
And I'll be your master.

Green gravel, green gravel, your grass is so green
You're the finest young maiden that ever I've seen
We washed her, we dried her, we dressed her in silk
And we wrote down her name with a golden pen
          and ink.
Oh Kathleen, Oh Kathleen your true love is dead
But we've sent you a letter to turn back your head.

There were other full length songs like 'Johnny Todd, Ah Ma,
All round the Loney O, I'll tell me Ma', and '**Fair** Rosa' but,
skipping songs and others to one side, the acting songs when the
girls acted out the plot in ring games were by far the best and
many's the time 'Poor Toby' was brought back to life or the
rival May queens and their supporters vied with each other.

Our queen can birl her leg
Birl her leg, birl her leg,
Our queen can birl her leg,
Birl her leg.

Our queen can smoke a feg
Smoke a feg, smoke a feg
Our queen can smoke a feg
Smoke a feg.

Our queen can eat a hard bap
Eat a hard bap, eat a hard bap
Our queen can eat a hard bap
Eat a hard bap.

Our queen up the river with your yah-yah-yah
Your queen down the river with your yah-yah-yah
Our queen up the river and we'll keep her there
    forever
With your yah-yah-yah-yah-yah.

Taunting songs were often exchanged between gangs:

Our wee Willie John,
His clothes are in the pawn,
He's up the spout, and he can't get out,
Our wee Willie John.

Ah poor oul Bendy,
Your bum is full of cendy.

Does your mammy know you're out,
Does your da drink stout,
Does your granny chew tobacco in the yard?

A common reply was 'Cry ba, cry ba, stick your finger in your
eye ba,' but mostly we boys confined our songs to parodying
hymns or advertising slogans.

Barney Hughes's bread,
It sticks to your belly like lead;
Not a bit of wonder

You fart like thunder,
Barney Hughes's bread.

Or as Fr McLoughlin conducted the hymn singing during confo (confraternity) in Clonard Monastery, a thousand boyish voices bawled with gusto:

Tonto Mergo make my hair grow.

I think Fr McLoughlin knew what we were at but he said nothing. God in Clonard, missions and retreats aside, was always good humoured. He still is.

On occasion we were moved to sing a rallying song as we sallied forth against Getty Street.

There's a big ship sailing up the alley, alley-oh,
The alley, alley-oh, the alley, alley-oh,
There's a big ship sailing up the alley, alley-oh,
On the last day of September.
Alley, alley-oh, alley, alley-oh,
The big ship sails away,
There's a big shipping sailing up the......

Rhymes were often made, in mocking fashion about names. I recall one:

Hi, Mrs Kelly
Would you speak to your wee Nellie,
For she hit me in the belly,
With a big lump of jelly.

A life long friend of mine who was temporarily nicknamed Geek, had to suffer the insulting chant of:

Poor oul Geek,
His head is full of keek.

Bad language was seldom used, and although most of the children's rhymes were hurtful for the victim, real harm was rarely intended. Apart from odd scuffles they usually received only the well-worn reply:

> Sticks and stones may break my bones,
> But names will never hurt me.

Big people were always referred to as so and so's mammy or daddy, brother or sister. Old people were known as mister or missus. Sometimes they were called oul ma so and so or oul da such and such, but that was always out of earshot of parents.

Grannies played a central part in rearing large families. Hugh Quinn vividly recalls such a lady.

> I once had a granny
> And songs she had many
> And there ne'er will be any
> Shall sing them so well
> Her face was all wrinkles
> But her eyes were all twinkles
> And her voice full of tinkles
> And clear as a bell.
>
> As she baked on the griddle
> Her tongue like a fiddle
> Lilted rum-tum-tum-tiddle
> Singing sweet songs as well.
>
> Of lovers who parted
> And fell broken-hearted
> She sang, till tears started
> And down her cheeks fell.
>
> Of soldiers and sailors
> Of tinkers and tailors
> Of ranters and railers
> I heard in a spell.
>
> As granny lay dying
> She said through her sighing
> 'Dear child! wheest your crying'
> Then bade me farewell.

I once had a granny
And songs she had many
And there ne'er will be any
Shall sing them so well.

Nicknames were common: Maguires always got Squire, Murphys — Spud, Whites were called Chalkie, boys with Mac in their name were invariably called Mackers while surnames were shortened and lengthened at will: Burnsie, Fernsie, Morgy, Scully, Doc.

Some names were passed down through generations, their meanings often lost in obscurity as in the case of Bendo McKee. Christian names were also distorted: Seán became Seánie; Alphonsus, Fonsus or Fonsie; Séamus, Séamie; Ciarán, Cernie; and so on. Those with odd mannerisms got suitable nicknames. One fellah in our class had the title of Guts Glaland, another Failey. All this led to some embarrassment when calling for companions, especially as their proper names were used only by close family and unknown to almost everybody else. Mothers did not always react well when a dirty faced urchin called asking, 'Is Cleaky allowed out?'

Sometimes we were curtly reminded that it was 'Terence you call him', and Terence, no doubt under severe maternal pressure, would tell us, until the notion or the pressure wore off, 'Don't be calling me that, m'da paid money for m'name'; or, 'I've a handle to my jug'.

Nicknames, of course, are universal, but all the same they seem to have a unique place in Belfast male camaraderie, passing into adulthood with their owners. In more recent years in prison, I discovered that eighty percent of the men had nicknames. Dipper, Breeze-Block, Hole-in-the-head, Doc, Dosser, Stew, Todler, Munky, Paddy Mo, Heavy Head, Crazy Joc, Rigor Mortis, Soppy Walter, Padre Pio, Dark, Ding Dong, Mr Sheen, Skin, Bangers, Paddy the Lad... the list is endless. And so too undoubtedly are their histories. But that's another story.

In the summer as we grew older, walks up to the Divis and Black Mountains became more and more frequent and whole days were spent exploring the caves or the forests. Looking back, the 'caves' were rather humble efforts and the 'forests' were far from grandiose affairs but even jaundiced hindsight cannot minimise the fun we had dodging and yelling through thick bushes or along little mountainy trails. On Sundays whole families made their way up the mountain lonnan, past the wee tin church, stopping for a drink at the river and away on up the windy track to the waterfall, where the real mountain started. The mountain lonnan meets the Ballygomartin Road at this point and a small whitewashed cottage sits at the junction. There are two paths, the lower skirting the base of the mountain and branching upwards at a number of points while the upper path reaches directly for 'the hatchet field' and 'the gully'.

A hundred yards above the whitewashed cottage, a huge jagged rock face stands the height of several stories of a building. We called it 'the riddley rock' and frightened ourselves by daring each other to scale it. Above were acres and acres of bracken and heather especially laid out for us to tumble through headlong, screaming and whooping with the sheer joy of being alive. We found wild strawberries once away towards Ligoniel and called the mountainy road 'strawberry path' ever afterwards. Likewise with 'running path', because of our inability to stop once we set off downwards. Behind 'the hatchet field', so called because of its shape, was 'the bottle field', which also got its name from its distinctive shape. Between them an acre of bluebells raised their heads amid heather and whin bushes.

As we became more adventurous we started to find less orthodox ways to the top. Straight up across the fields behind Beechmount, past the Springfield Dam with its resident swans and its seasonal epidemic of spricks or tadpoles, and up by the Rock Dam to arrive hot and flushed through the loose shale which always presented an extra challenge. At times we cut from Colin Glen right up, splashing and scrambling along the river to Turnaroy and climbed beyond Hannahstown to arrive at the gully from its opposite side. In recent times such outings seem to have lost their popularity. The combined forces of television, the British Army and a partition of barbed wire rising from behind the waterfall seem to have made 'the mountain' something for looking up at. Looking down, other than from spyholes or dug-outs, appears to be a thing of the past.

The views were always panoramic, stretching towards the Mournes — 'if you can see them it's going to rain, if you can't it's raining' — or in the other direction the Castlereagh

Hills; while below us Belfast sprawled towards the shipyards. Behind, over the mountain, on a good day Lough Neagh shimmered in the distance; we walked there a few times and caused parental panic once when a hike took us in the opposite direction along the range of low hills to McArt's Fort and the Cave Hill. We arrived home after dark, via the Antrim Road, singing and tired and totally unprepared for the crisis which our prolonged absence had created.

Holidays away from Belfast were unknown and anyway we didn't need them — every boyish whim could be fulfilled within yards or miles of our own front doors. Day outings to Bangor, Crawfordsburn, Greencastle or Bellevue Zoo were family affairs, organised in conjunction with a clan of cousins, and with parental control placing its restraints on our exploits and behaviour.

A few pennies from uncles or aunts helped to defray candy-apple or gobstopper expenses on our return, and Patsy's corner shop or Stinker Greenwood's was always first port-of-call. After such outings a visit to Malachy Morgan's Supper Saloon, with its gaping aquarium of goldfish, provided an economical and speedy fish supper; but Longs, famous in Belfast for its fish and chips, was really the place for such grub and still provides a special treat, having survived both redevelopment and the war.

No doubt, then as now, there were broken marriages, drunken husbands and great poverty but we were unaffected, by and large, by such mundane things. They were nothing to do with us and we were too busy to have anything to do with them. That this would change was inevitable but the loss of innocence which comes with the arrival of maturity was staved off by the many diversions which each new day brought. Our front doors, with their little scrubbed half moons of pavement, the wee streets beyond and the mountains behind were our playground. But now the wee streets are gone and with them whole generations of childhood games and customs.

Bunking In

A little child
Kicking a stone
Going to the pictures
All alone.

The years have flown
And all alone
A man is left
Kicking a stone.
      (with apologies to) *Nora Hill*

THE trolley buses whirred their way past us as we queued in a long straggling line for the matinée in Clonard picture house.

'Do youse think we cud bunk our way in, when your man's not lukin'?' asked Josie McMenamy, nudging my attention towards the usher who stood Horatio-like in the foyer.

'You've two hopes,' said Jamesie Magee casting an experienced eye along the line, 'Bob Hope and no hope. Your man knollered two wee bucks last week and barred the two of them, so he did.'

'Awh, they walked right into it!' Josie scoffed. 'I stud here and I knew they were going to get knollered the way they were going about it. Your man was blimping right at them when they made their move. Stands to reason, doesn't it, that you'll get caught trying stupid things. Now, I reckon if his attention was distracted two of us cud sneaky-beaky in past him.'

'And how could you distract his attention?'

'Well, when the line gets down close to him and when me and him is talking, youse two can nip in.'

'Do you think we came up the Lagan in a bubble?' I retorted. 'You're dead fly, Josie: me and Jamesie's the ones who'll get caught.'

'You'll not get caught', said Josie. 'Your man is nuts about pigeons, and if I ask him about that new tumbler me da's got he'll be so mesmerised telling me the whole ins and outs of it that you'll be in before he knows what's hit him.'

'I'm not too keen on it', said Jamesie. 'I wudn't like to miss the big picture.'

'Ah, stop your whingeing', Josie interrupted. 'We'll be able to split the spondooliks between us — a three-way split. Okay? And you'll see the big picture, and the wee one, for nothing.'

'I don't see why it has to be in a three-way split', Jamesie grumbled. 'I mean to say, we're taking all the risks, you shud only be getting a wing.'

'Ah, be a brick, Jamesie, don't be gurning now. We'll work it out after. Sure we're nearly there now. Are youse game?'

'Aye', we agreed as the crowd jostled its way past the gateway and towards the ticket box. Minutes later me and Jamesie stood in the rain at the corner of Leeson Street. We glared at the spot where Josie McMenamy had disappeared into the friendly innards of Clonard.

'I'll knock his pan in when I see him', scowled Jamesie as he gingerly touched his backside. 'Your man nearly ruined my marriage prospects. Wait till I get that wee gett Josie, him and his "What do you think my da should feed his new pigeon on, mister?" I thought your man was going to murder us.'

'Awh well,' said I, 'sure it wasn't a very good picture anyway. I saw the coming attractions and it looked desperate. Let's go for a wee dander. Next time we'll make Josie sneak in and we'll talk to your man.'

'It's always the same with me', Jamesie complained as we dandered up Dunlewey Street to Mrs Rooney's. 'I knew things weren't going to work out and yet Josie talked me into it, so he did. I'm as thick as champ, so I am. Our Paddy says if I had any sense I'd be a half-wit.'

'Ach, it's not as bad as all that', I said. 'I mean to say,

Clonard picture house.

like, it cud have been worse. I mean your man cud have barred us altogether. Like, he caught us fair and square and he just give us a good boot, and that was that. Like, I thought my tonsils were going to come out my throat.' I laughed in a feeble effort to cheer Jamesie up.

'Oh, I don't know', he persisted. 'You'll be laughing at the other side of your face next Saturday when your man shows us the road home.'

'Well if you're going to be gurning all day I'm getting some honeycomb and some mixed-ups and I'm going home right this minute.'

'Okay, okay,' Jamesie conceded, 'don't be getting your knickers in a twist. I was only saying, like, here we are out here in the rain and Josie McMenamy, the fly wee slabber, is in watching the pictures. But if you're going to take it out on me, well, we'd be better forgetting the whole episode so we wud.'

'All right', I said as we went into Mrs Rooney's to spend our picture money, 'just put it down to experience.'

Later, as me and Jamesie divided our sweeties in the summer house of a deserted and rain-swept Dunville Park, we pondered on the part that fate and Josie McMenamy had played in our lives.

'It seems to me', said Jamesie, 'that me and you always come off the worst.'

'Ach, not all the times,' I countered, 'I mean to say, Josie's not the worst and he did save you from that wee tin gang from Getty Street a couple of times.'

'Aye, but that was only because he wanted to cog my ecker. If he thinks he's going to do that again he's another think coming.'

'And what about the way he always gets us the buns off his uncle who works in Hughes's?'

'Aye, well, that's true enough,' said Jamesie wistfully, 'I wudn't mind one of them snowballs and a Paris bun right now.'

'Or a diamond and a sorehead', I added moving up on the damp wooden seat. 'C'mon and we'll go on home. I'm starving.'

'Me too. My belly thinks my throat's cut. But we'd better wait till the pictures get out. I hope your man doesn't tell me da the score. He'll kill me. We better wait for a wee while yet.'

'It must be nearly tea-time now. I'm looking forward to a big fry — a dipped soda and a fried egg would be smashing.'

'Don't think about it', Jamesie suggested. 'If you think about it, it only makes you worse. Let's take a dander down the road and by that time they shud be out.'

'Dead on', said I, glad to be out of the summer house now that the sweets were done. 'C'mon and we'll have a race to the gate.'

Down at the Clonard as we arrived the matinée crowds were beginning to stream out into the light drizzling rain. Jamesie and I took shelter at the corner of Spinner Street as we watched for Josie McMenamy to come our way.

'Remember,' said Jamesie, his murderous mood returning, 'remember the time he wanted us to rob the orchie up the Glen Road. He nearly got us killed that time as well.'

'So he did', said I, 'thon big dog nearly ate me.'

'I know', said Jamesie. 'I'm never going to listen to one word Josie ever says again. He's far too sleekit. Remember that time: ''Just give us a wee scoutsie up the tree and I'll shake off a pile of apples'' he said. Aye, dead on. He was safe up the tree when the dog made a go at us. Well, this is me finished with his wee schemes.'

At that Josie approached us, cheerfully splashing his way through a puddle of rainwater. 'Bully, Jamesie', he said. 'Okay our kid,' he greeted me, 'youse made a right mess of that. Youse are two chancers. If I knew youse weren't serious I wudn't have made the effort.'

'What do you mean?' we both exploded indignantly. 'Its you that messed it up. We never had a chance.'

'You're supposed to run', said Josie. 'Once you get in he never gets you and he can't leave his place long enough to try. I mean to say, youse were like two oul dolls at a funeral.'

'We'll soon see whose funeral it is if you keep on like that, Josie McMenamy', said Jamesie darkly, taking a pace forward.

'Ah, catch yourself on, wee buck', said Josie. 'I'm only slegging. You can't even take a geg now. Well, have it your own way. It was a desperate picture anyway. I'm away on home. Youse coming? C'mon and we'll call in and see our Tommy. He told me to call for a few buns.'

We glared at him sullenly. 'All right', he said. 'It's your own funeral, it's all the same difference to me.'

'Okay,' I said, 'sure it's on our way home; c'mon Jamesie.'

We set off together, Jamesie reluctantly bringing up the rear and glaring at Josie.

'Wait till you see the size of the gravy rings you get on a Saturday', Josie enthused.

'You'd think you were the only one ever got gravy rings', said Jamesie sourly.

'Well, one sure thing. I'm the only one here has the picture money left,' said Josie, 'and the way you're carrying on I don't know whether to split it or not.'

We stopped dead in our tracks. 'What do you mean?' I asked. 'You haven't still got the picture money, have you?'

'Aye', said Josie with a grin. 'When your man was busy kicking youse two out I just dandered on in.'

'Well, you dirty rat', said I in amazement. 'You're dead lucky.'

'Let's see it', said Jamesie grudgingly.

'Disbelieving Thomas,' returned Josie, 'you'll see it in the shop.'

'Three-way split, Josie', we shouted charging after him.

'Last one in's a dodo!', he yelled over his shoulder and we dashed acorss the road. Later, strolling down Leeson Street, with our bellies full of buns and poke full of sweets, just in time for our tea, Jamesie stopped at the corner of Cairns Street.

'You know,' he reflected, 'it wasnt such a bad day after all. Was the big picture really stinking?' he asked Josie.

'Desperate altogether', said Josie. 'I'll see youse after tea and tell youse all about it. Youse'll be glad youse didn't get in when youse hear the score. The fella got killed in the end', he added as we arrived at the corner.

'See youse in half an hour', said Jamesie.

'Okay', we replied.

'Hould on a wee minute. do youse fancy sneaking up into me da's pigeon shed?' asked Josie. 'He'll never hear us if we go over Ma Delaney's yard wall.'

'I don't know', said Jamesie.

'It's a dead cinch', said Josie. 'Oul Ma Delaney's stone deaf and we'd be nice and dry.'

'It's still a wee bit dodgy.'

'No problem', interrupted Josie, 'and I'll get some mineral to bring with us. Are youse game?'

'Okay', I said, 'what about you Jamesie?'

'Aye, I suppose so', said Jamesie reluctantly. 'Mind you, I'm not going first.'

'Sure, we'll see about that later', replied Josie.

'See you.'

'See youse', concluded Jamesie, 'and Josie, don't be forgetting about the mineral, will you?'

Snake Belts and Dog Fights

And everywhere, in street and square
We're always on parade
As we march in style and Indian file
The Scavengers' Brigade.

Belfast Ballad

I CUT up from Smithfield Pet Shop with a new dog lead and collar and headed for Balaclava Street where I was to meet Josie and Jamesie. It was a Saturday morning and we were set for a game of handball at Raglan Street. I met them as arranged and we went off through the area.

'Any odds on you?' Jamesie asked.

'Nawh', said I, 'I had to cadge the money for Rory's new lead.'

'I'm skint', Josie grunted.

A group of girls making their way towards us, on the opposite side of the street, began giggling and whispering as we approached. As we passed they turned and followed, breaking into a noisy chorus.

'Our Josie's Sadie's wee duck,

Sadie's wee duck, Sadie's wee duck,
Our Josie's Sadie's wee duck,
Sadie's wee quack, quack, quack!'

Josie scowled and with a reddener turned angrily and threw an empty tin at them.

'Skeedaddle', he yelled. 'Piss away off.'

They retired a little bit, shouting and laughing, but continued to follow us at a distance and to taunt Josie, who looked decidedly scundered by the whole affair.

'What's all that about?' I asked.

'Did you not hear?' grinned Jamesie, 'Josie's got a girl so he has. Why do you think he's skint? Two seats in the back stalls that's why. Isn't it Josie, oul mate?'

'I haven't got a girl', Josie scowled fiercely. 'And don't be starting something you can't finish.'

'That's not what I heard', said Jamesie innocently, 'I heard you and Sadie's going steady and that...'

'We're not going to get a game of handball with that mob behind us', I interrupted, 'let's go on up the road instead.'

'Okay', they agreed, both glad, I think, at the prospect of getting rid of our noisy entourage.

'I'll met youse at the shelters. I'm going to run on and get Rory. I'll try on his new lead.'

I left them to lose Josie's tormenters and later, free of female followers, we strolled up the Sprinky. 'Let's cut down through the brickie', Jamesie suggested as we passed the West Circular Road.

'What about Rory?' I queried. 'Westrock's alive with dogs and he's sure to get into a fight.'

'Don't worry', sneered Jamesie, 'sure you can carry him. C'mon.'

Josie and he set off and I trailed behind them, holding Rory on a tight leash and warning him about the canine risks which lay ahead in the bungalows. The brickfields stretched before us, with the pithead to our left. Underfoot, huge disused brick-kilns carved tunnels in all directions with cavernous holes appearing at will where tunnels had collapsed. I had just caught up on Josie and Jamesie when suddenly a large stone smashed off a rusting oil can in front of us. We stopped, startled as another heaker whizzed over our heads. 'Don't move, just hold your horses and walk over this way, and don't try any funny business', a voice commanded.

We looked around uncertainly to find we were surrounded on all sides by a group of dirty-faced boys of our own age who had appeared from underground and were now slowly closing in on us. 'Right lads,' the voice guldered, 'quit the clodding, bring them down to the den.

Still speechless and a little shaken we were shepherded towards a large kiln from which the voice echoed. Inside, by the side of a pile of smoking rubbish, its owner awaited us. He was a big tousle-headed youth with buck teeth and a wide grin. 'Sit down', he told us. We remained standing. 'Who owns the wee pup?' he asked.

'He does', said Jamesie.

'What age is it?'

'Six months', replied Jamesie eagerly.

'Awh, a nice wee dog.' He called Rory towards him offering successfully as a bribe a piece of Jacob's cream cracker. 'And a new lead as well.'

'Where youse from?'

'Down the road', I replied.

'Well, we're from Tintown and this is our territory. Isn't that right lads?' The lads chorused their assent. 'And nobody', he continued, 'but nobody from down the road or anywhere else comes into our territory unless we say so. Now sit down!'

We sat down. He offered us a cream cracker. 'We get them in the pithead. You have to watch for the lorries coming and get in quick before the rats and the seagulls. The pithead's our territory as well', he added meaningfully. 'We ride the gypsies' horses over there. Here, try one of these crackers. They're really gorgeous. G'wan, try one.'

We refused, all except Rory who sucked round his new benefactor with so much tail wagging that I was sickened by the sight of him. 'I think I'll keep the dog for letting youse through here. All right?' he addressed me. My protests were cut off by a chorus of threats from the rest of our captors.

'Put the dog on the fire, Mackers.'

'Don't let him slabber to you like that. Knock his balls in!'

'Can you fight?' said Mackers.

'I don't know', I replied, eyeing his superior build.

'Well, I'll tell you what', he offered, 'Jimmy here,' he pointed to Jimmy who grinned back, 'Jimmy here's not really in our gang yet. He's still to do the last test. I think you and him should have a fair go. And if he wins he comes into the gang and I keep the dog. And if you win he doesn't and you keep the dog. Okay? That's fair, isn't it?' he turned to his comrades who, along with Jamesie, shouted their agreement.

Seconds later me and Jimmy faced each other in a small cleared pit while the rest of them, captives and captors alike, lined the edge above us. The captors yelled encouragement to Jimmy, their champion. The captives, I noticed, remained silent, while Rory ignored me totally and gave all his attention to Mackers and his dwindling supply of cream crackers.

After the first few quick seconds of physical and psychological byplay Jimmy made a lunge at me. To my surprise when I stepped back he fell heavily to the ground, knocking his knee painfully in the process. I leaped on his back, kicked at the injured knee. He, for his part, started to cry loudly, shocking me and drawing the fire of his outraged comrades. 'Let him up', commanded Mackers. 'You won', he congratulated me, handing back Rory who returned reluctantly to where I panted and perspired with relief. 'Just before youse go', said Mackers, 'have youse any odds?'

'No', we chorused.

'Well, have youse any anything?' We shook our heads. 'I think I'll hold on to the dog's lead.' Mackers pondered. 'Nawh, a deal's a deal. Anyway it wudn't fit any of our lurchers.' He eyed Josie and Jamesie. 'C'm'ere', he instructed Jamesie, 'give's your belt.' he scowled. Jamesie reluctantly started to separate his belt from his trousers. Mackers, unimpressed by the speed of this operation, scrutinised him from close quarters. 'Don't I know you from somewhere?' he asked. 'Weren't you with the wee bucks who knocked off the oil cloth and tea chests from our bonfire last August?'

'Who, me?' Jamesie stammered. 'No chance, honest to God, Mackers. No chance was it me.'

He handed over the belt. Mackers continued to eye him closely.

'Nawh', he said finally. 'Maybe it wasn't you. Anyway,' he grinned, 'thanks for the belt. That's all of us happy now. Away youse go.' We were escorted a few yards away from the den. 'Don't be coming up this way again', Mackers warned. 'Stay down the road where yis belong. Remember, this is Tintown territory.'

We made our way in silence across the brickie towards the bungalows. Underfoot we could hear Mackers' men as they shadowed us, below ground, through the brick kilns. None of us spoke till we got to Westrock Drive. I held Rory's lead tightly as we made our way through the bungalows.

'What about my new snake belt?' Jamesie grumbled.

'What about it', I retorted. 'That's your hard lines.'

'You know', said Josie, 'what my granny used to always say?' We dandered down towards the back of Riddels field.

'What was that?' I asked.

'It makes the devil laugh to see the biter bit', he replied. 'Isn't that right, Jamesie?' Jamesie clutched his trousers and said nothing as we made our way down the road and homewards for our tea.

Wakes and Witches

One night in wild November
When shrill wind whistled high
And street lamps shimmered blue and dim
I heard the Banshee cry.

Hugh Quinn

AT times we were taken to a wake house to stand, awkward and afraid, by the side of a coffin gazing wide-eyed at the remains of a neighbour or relative. The body would be laid out in the back room or bedroom, hands clasped, with rosary beads twined through cold dead fingers.

'Isn't she a lovely corpse?' old women would whisper as they stood up slowly from kneeling in prayer to put a Mass card on the coffin.

'She looks just like herself, it's a mercy from God she went when she did. Ach, Jimmy, I didn't see you when I came in. I'm sorry for your trouble. How's your father taking it?'

'He's lying down, Mrs McLaverty, he's done in with sitting up last night. He'll be sorry he's missed you.'

'Awh, don't be worrying about that. Sure, youse have enough to worry youse, God knows. I was just saying to Sarah that your mother looks just like herself. Thank God she had a happy death. She had a hard life altogether and didn't she go downhill desperate this last six months. I was only talking to her the other week. I got a quare gunk when I saw her and I said so as well and she said to me, ''Sure I'll be out again once the good weather comes in.'' God knows, there she is now. Sure, you never know when you'll be sent for.'

'That's true, Mrs McLaverty, but as you say it was a mercy God took her when He did. And she had a happy death just like she'd always prayed for. The priest was here, me da and all of us and our Seán just got in from Manchester an hour before she went. She just gave a wee sigh in her sleep and a wee smile and that was that. You wouldn't have known she died at all.'

'Ach, Jimmy, she looks like she's sleeping yet. God rest her soul. That's the road we'll all be going and it's lucky them that has their family around them at the end. I'll go down now, Jimmy, I see more people coming in. Why don't you put your head down for a wee while yourself, Jimmy, you look done in.'

'Oh, I'm all right, Mrs McLaverty. Come down the stairs and have a wee cup of tea. Sadie's in the back. She'll be glad to see you.'

'Well, I'll just go down for a wee minute, don't be troubling yourself about the tea. I'll get a wee cup in my hand before I go. I told Harry I'd be up again to let him come down. We only got the news this morning. Maggie Ritchie told me on the way to Mass and Harry saw it in the death notices. I'll just say another wee prayer before I go down.'

We stood through all this, shifting awkwardly from foot to foot, jingling the few coppers that were pressed upon us on such occasions and avoiding the eyes of other equally well scrubbed boys who were brought in also by parents or grandparents to say a prayer before being released to whisper in a wee group outside the door. Inside, neighbours and relatives gathered to talk and pray, swapping yarns and recollections about the dead person. The family were kept busy making sandwiches and serving biscuits and tea with a limited supply of stout or sherry for those who preferred supping to sipping. On occasion the crowd would spill over into the hallway and onto the street. Until we were sent or brought home to bed we listened to and watched with some awe and puzzlement the rituals which accompanied death. And rituals there were in plenty.

The clocks were stopped at the exact time of the deceased's passing, blinds were drawn, black crêpe was fastened to the front door, mirrors were covered with white cloth and the window of the death room was opened to permit the spirit to make its escape unimpeded. This, we were told, took four hours.

The corpse was washed by one or more of the neighbours (often an old woman who served also as midwife) and then it was dressed in the robe of some sacred order. The remains were never left alone until the coffin was taken to the chapel on the night before the funeral Mass and on the way from the chapel to the cemetery an effort was made to ensure that the cortège, which always took the longest route, passed near the family home. The coffin was taken out of the house feet first. I learned later that this was done because the small halls and narrow stairways meant that the coffin had to be stood upright on its way down the stairs. Understandably enough, it was considered better to stand the corpse on its feet than on its head.

The coffin was carried on its final journey, feet foremost, shoulder high or in a hearse. Neighbours, relatives and friends took turns at taking a lift. I recall an American visitor being asked 'Do you want a lift?' He, in anticipation of being driven back from the cemetery, replied 'Yeah' and was startled to be hurriedly ushered to the front of the cortège to take his place with three others under the heavy coffin. Not to get a lift was considered an insult. In chapel the coffin was placed with the corpse's feet facing the altar. For some strange reason this practice was reversed for priests who were carried head first and placed facing the altar in the same position.

Some people placed a bowl of salt under the coffin during the wake in the belief that this kept the body from smelling and many kept the door crêpe because of its power to cure. Once when I asked an undertaker if he knew of any superstition associated with wakes he told me that some people were reluctant to shake hands with him while others considered it good luck. His wife told me that many poor people believed that the dead don't rest until the funeral account is paid.

As we got older we would call, for a dare, on our own to a wake house and ask, 'Missus, can we come in and see the dead?' Once in, the ultimate mark of courage was actually to touch the corpse. No one seemed to think it disrespectful for us to behave in such a manner; perhaps they recalled their own childhood curiosity. Death was accepted with quiet faith as the inevitable and definite conclusion facing all. It was to be questioned only when it was sudden, violent or when it affected the young.

Apart from the yarns told in the wake house itself attendance at a wake, for us, always rekindled the ghost story telling sessions at Harbinson's corner. There, as the gas lamps cast their circular glow along the deserted streets, we gathered on our hunkers to be frightened by the tales of ghosts, bogeymen, banshees and the devil himself. Stories of banshees appearing, or dogs howling before a death, of deaths coming in threes, of the haunted house in Cairns Street or strange occurrences in Lincoln Street I could take. The headless nun of the Giant's Foot and the old woman we suspected of being a witch were a wee bit more scary but not half as bad as even the mention of the devil. He was a different matter altogether; and I found him most frightening because of his ability to appear in human form. Accounts of such appearances were well recorded, and in some instances were substantiated by examples of local men whose hair had turned white at the very sight of him. I remember clearly the night Josie told us of the experience which once befell his father.

'Me da', Josie began, 'was playing cards with his mates one night at the watchman's hut up in the brickie. They were playin' poker, with a penny a stake, around the fire when this man came up and asked them cud he take a hand. Well, nobody knew him but oul Jimmy, that's the watchman, had seen him a few times on the road, so they said, "Okay, pull up to the fire", and they dealt him into the game.

'Anyway, they went on playing and talking, having a bit of crack and paying little or no attention to their cards, especially when your man, the stranger, told them a yarn or two about foreign countries and about his life as a seaman. He had a big carton of cigarettes which he passed around and a wee flask of brandy. Anyway, Jimmy the watchman seemed to be getting a wee bit annoyed, like, me da says that's because Jimmy was on a winning streak until your man arrived, although me da said Jimmy wasn't a bit shy about taking his share of the fags and a big slug of the brandy.

'Anyway, when me da saw Jimmy getting crabbity, he started to deal out the cards again and one of them fell off the oul board they were using and landed on the ground. Me da bent down to pick it up and out of the tail of his eye he caught a wee geek of your man's feet. And do you want me to tell you something? Your man had a cloven hoof instead of a foot. Me da was so scared that he jumped up on his two hind legs and shouted, "Jesus, Mary and Joseph!" He knocked the oul board over he was so scared. And you know what? Your man just got up and smiled at them all. They were terrified out of their lives. Your man turned around and walked away from them and you want to know something? They cud hear his foot clop-clop-clopping the whole way down the street.'

Afterwards I relived such stories in the shadows on the back bedroom wall. Once my granny had to take me into her bed where she admonished me before I slipped off into an uneasy sleep. 'That's an end to that oul carry-on up at the corner. There'll be no more gallivanting about at night from now on for you, wee lad. From now on you'll be in your own bed as soon as it gets dark. I don't know what's come over me, letting you get your head filled with such nonsense.'

For all that, nonsense or otherwise, older people treated such matters with respect. The house was always blessed with holy water at bedtime; bread, water and salt were laid out on the hearth on All Souls' Night; and a dream about a dead person meant that he or she needed prayers. If the dead person smiled in the dream, there was the consolation that they, at least, were happy.

Many older people also believed in the fairies. Tradition had it that there was a fairy well and a fairy thorn down in Divis Street where St Comgall's School stands. Up at the Giant's Foot, a local landmark, so called because once upon a time the imprint of a giant foot could be seen, was another fairy thorn and a fairy ring. There was also a fairy well in the Bog Meadows while down towards the bottom of Divis Street was the site of a healing well.

A few old people also had healing powers, while some could read dreams and others cards or tea leaves. There were always misgivings voiced about spilling salt, which meant tears; or coal falling from the fire on to the hearth, an announcement of strange visitors. Bad luck came not only from walking under ladders but from all kinds of obscure happenings such as an umbrella unfurled in the house or boots on a table. A St Brigid's cross, with moral backing from a horse shoe, protected most houses.

Walking in cow's clap or dog's dirt was good luck, provided you didn't tramp it into the house. An itchy left hand meant you were going to come into some money and prompted the following words and action:

> Rub it on wood
> Make it come true.

This occasionally, if a sceptic was in the vicinity, drew a quick reply:

> Rub it on your ass,
> Make it come fast.

Cures, half ritualistic and half medicinal were many and varied for all kinds of afflictions from warts to boils. Relics, bread poultices, holy water and strange condiments were often pressed into service. Children with whooping cough were passed three times under a donkey's belly or, more practically perhaps, escorted to the gasworks where they inhaled a daily dose of the air around the huge gas holders.

By such means life was protected and when it expired a happy death and a debtless send-off to the other world was, for most older people, a much prayed-for and greatly desired conclusion to lives spent from birth to grave in the same house, in the same street, in the same district. 'They would all meet again, God willing, in the next world.' That much at least was certain, in a world of meal-to-meal existence. As one old man told me, 'Well, of course, I hope to go to heaven, but that's a decision which rests with the man above. Anyway,' he added with a grin, 'I'm sure I've plenty of friends in both places.'

Prods and Micks

O the bricks they will bleed and the rain it
    will weep
And the damp Lagan fog lull the city to sleep;
It's to hell with the future and live on the past
May the Lord in his mercy be kind to Belfast.

Maurice James Craig

'ARE you a Prod?' he challenged me. 'Are you a Prod or a Mick?' There were three of them, the biggest one acting as interrogator while the other two blocked my exit.

'I'm an Irish Catholic', I replied, indifferent even at that early age to the Roman prefix and with visions of boy martyrs uppermost in my juvenile mind. 'I'm a Catholic', I proudly re-affirmed, safe in the knowledge that they must be also, seeing as we were in the middle of Divis Street, just below St Comgall's School. Had we been in more hostile territory the cock might well have crowed thrice, but here on home ground being a Catholic was safe enough.

'Where do you live?'

'That's none of your business', I replied, seeing over his shoulder a group of women shoppers coming in our direction and, I hoped, to my rescue.

'Is it not?' He grabbed me by the shirt front and my confidence vanished as he pushed his face close to mine and the women dandered by, oblivious to my plight.

'Give him a hiding, Jimmy', one of my assailant's smaller runny-nosed confederates encouraged. 'He's a sally rod, give him the head. Knock his melt in.'

'Where do you live, wee buck?' Jimmy asked me again.

'Abercorn Street', said I, discretion winning the day. 'Abercorn Street North, number fifteen.'

'Make him say the Our Father', said snattery-nose.

'I'm not saying the Our Father for you,' said I, 'I'll get my da for youse if you don't let me go. Wait till I get home.'

'You're not going home', scowled Jimmy. 'We don't like Prods, and you look like a Prod.'

'So he does,' chirped in the third inquisitor, 'look at his eyes, they're like wee marleys, so they are. Make him say the Our Father.'

'No, make him say the Hail Mary. Prods say the Our Father, they say that art in Heaven, instead of who art in Heaven, but they don't believe in Our Lady, so make him say the Hail Mary.'

I mentally reheased the five sorrowful mysteries and an act of contrition. Panic was setting in as dusk settled and my captors became more menacing. Thoughts of Dominic Savio vanished.

'Okay,' said Jimmy, 'say the Hail Mary.'

I dutifully complied, tears welling up and a lump in my throat doing its best to mix me up. He released my shirt front and his two companions, disappointed, stared over my head.

'Do you smoke?' asked snattery-nose. 'I'm dying for a fag. C'mon, give us your odds.'

I gave them a thrupenny bit, a sprassy and a miraculous medal before being released to run, tears tripping me, the short way home. That was my first contact with sectarianism, albeit of a minor kind; but all the same it, like all sectarianism, had nothing to do with religion and was merely, as always, a profitable ruse, in this case for providing Woodbines. The spot where our transaction took place, though I didn't know it then, had long been the scene of sectarian faction fights, the most serious of them taking place only a few yards from us, in what was once a brickfield separating the Falls from the Shankill Road.

Rioting in Belfast between factions has been traced back to 1835 and most local historians mention the years 1843, 1857, 1864, 1872, 1880, 1884 and 1886 as being the most serious.

In earlier contrast to this, Belfast had been the centre in the 1790s of an Irish political movement that linked Antrim and Down with the republics of France and America. As is commonly known and as Andrew Boyd observes in his *Holy War in Belfast,* Belfast's citizens celebrated the Fall of the Bastille, drank toasts to Mirabeau and Lafayette, and studied Paine's great book, *The Rights of Man.* Belfast Presbyterians formed the Society of United Irishmen and in the rebellion of 1798 fought alongside their Catholic neighbours for national independence and political democracy. In the old republican plot erected in 1912 in Milltown Cemetery were inscribed the names of upwards of twenty Protestant soldiers of the republic while the bodies of Henry Joy McCracken and other United Irishmen lie in Clifton Street Cemetery.

Yet within two generations the majority of Presbyterians had completely abandoned their revolutionary principles, embraced the politics of the Tories and developed a deep-rooted antipathy towards their Catholic neighbours. This transformation, as Boyd correctly states, is one of the most disturbing facts in Irish history. It was caused directly by the forces of reaction, supported by the wealthy landlord class, who feared the union of Catholic, Protestant and Dissenter. As Hugh Boulter, Lord Chief Justice, warned the London government in the eighteenth century, such a union would mean 'farewell to the English influence in this country'.

The Presbyterians, then as now, were the largest religious denomination apart from the Catholics. Had they remained untouched by the neo-fascism of Orangeism they would, in alliance with their Catholic countrymen, have undoubtedly transformed Irish society. They were, however, deeply divided, one faction headed by Thomas Cooke, a narrow-minded Paisley-type Tory, the other led by Henry Montgomery, a liberal whose father had been an officer in the battle of Antrim in 1798. Montgomery made no secret of his liberal political and religious principles. He campaigned for Catholic emancipation, was proud of his republican background and forthright in theological and political disputes with Cooke. Cooke, who was equally forthright in his views, was deeply anti-Catholic; and one of his ancestors had fought on the Williamite side during the wars at the end of the seventeenth century. He hated the United Irishmen and their democratic separatist principles and campaigned for control of Ireland's Presbyterians. He found support among the Tories, the landowning class and the Orange lodges and eventually succeeded in ousting Montgomery who left the parent church and formed the non-subscribing Presbyterian Church.

Cooke, secure in leadership of the Presbyterian Church, built up a powerful politico-religious movement in which the Orange order, by then nearly forty years in existence, was to play a major part. The Orange order, an exclusively Protestant and bitterly anti-Catholic organisation, had been formed in 1795 to protect poorer Protestant farmers and rich Protestant landlords; it was an alliance of the landed gentry and those poorer Protestants who were united in their distrust of liberalism and Irish Catholics. Until Cooke's time the Orange order had made little impact on the Presbyterians, and the first Orangemen were mainly descendants of the English rather than the Scottish planters. Under Cooke this situation changed dramatically and the Presbyterians were drawn increasingly away from radicalism to Toryism and the political cult of Orangeism. Political and religious bigotry of the most extreme description were fused together and, as the power of Orangeism increased Belfast saw the first of the riots with which we are so familiar to the present day.

The scene of many of these riots was to be West Belfast and as far back as 1843 the *Northern Whig* reported:

> One corner of our town, including a part of Sandy Row and Barrack Street, has been the theatre of much excitement and rioting, the contending parties being Catholics. and Protestants of a low description.

In 1847, the Pound Loney was the scene of protracted street fighting, with the Orangemen and the partisan town police force, egged on by Thomas Drew, an Orange demagogue, engaging in gunfights with the residents of the Loney area. Streets well known in recent times were mentioned regularly in reports from that period, and places like Durham Street, Millfield, Cullingtree Road, Grosvenor Road, the Boyne Bridge (then the Saltwater Bridge), Quadrant Street,

Albert Street and Leeson Street were but some of those featured.

Then as now, residents doused street lights to confuse police and military raiding parties. Bricks and pavers were used as weapons, street and area defence committees were formed, and gunfire was heard regularly. The July period became an annual occasion of disorder, often incited by mob orators such as Cooke, Drew or Hugh 'Roaring' Hanna, which spread on occasions to the shipyards and to Carrick Hill, Ballymacarrett, North Queen Street and Millfield. All these riots were marked by deaths, by the burning of public houses and by an exodus of working-class families into 'safer' areas.

In 1872 there was one particularly bloody encounter; later to be known as the battle of the brickfields, it took place a few days after a nationalist parade up the Falls Road. This was probably the first nationalist parade in Belfast since 1798 and was attended by about 30,000 people who assembled at Hannahstown to demand home rule and the release of the Fenian prisoners. The right of nationalists to march was opposed, as it has been to the present day, by force, and the parade was attacked at the Divis Street end of the Falls from the brickfields by a mob from the Shankill armed with guns, bricks, bottles and clubs. After a pitched battle, the attack was beaten off and the parade continued peacefully. However, sporadic fighting broke out between rival factions in different parts of the town and continued over the next few days. One vicious fight, involving about 3,000 people in Cullingtree Road, broke out and spread to Leeson Street and Lincoln Street, with a number of attempts being made to invade the Loney from both Sandy Row and the Shankill and sporadic gunfights breaking out across the open ground between these areas. On 18 August the battle of the brickfields was only one of a number of riots that shook Belfast. It began around three o'clock when about fifty armed men were spotted sneaking from the Shankill across the brickfields towards the Falls. The alarm was given in the Loney from where other armed men appeared and a gun battle commenced, in the course of which a counter-attack was launched from the Falls up Dover Street towards the Shankill. At the end of the day 'peace' was restored when British infantry camped on the brickfields.

Such occurrences became a regular if regrettable part of life through the nineteenth and early twentieth centuries; but in

Ancient Order of Hibernians Hall, Falls Road.

the 'fifties and early 'sixties going back and forth along Divis Street none of us thought of such things. Our parents and grandparents shopped regularly on the Shankill or in Sandy Row — there was a wider choice of shops and a better chance of a bargain. I even joined a boxing club for a few weeks, beside the Eagle Supper Saloon above Peter's Hill, at the foot of the Shankill Road, and none of us thought it odd that there were five Protestant churches in our midst and another on the Glen Road. There were, indeed, more Protestant than Catholic churches on the road. The church at Iveagh just above Broadway, on the front of the Falls Road, drew a sizeable congregation until recently, but the one on the Glen has turned its coat and now serves as a Catholic chapel, while the congregations of the others disappeared as a result of the shifts in population caused by the current troubles and redevelopment.

I was surprised therefore in my youth to be knocked back for a part-time job by a genial Orangeman who told me pleasantly, 'I'm sorry, son, but we don't employ your sort here. Cudn't do it. You dig with the wrong fut.' Although taken aback, I wasn't long catching on. It was the name of the school that did it, on top of my home address. Later, in my mid-teens, I worked for a few months in a pub beside the Shankill, on the Old Lodge Road. The clientèle were working class Protestants from the neighbouring streets with a sprinkling of Catholics. The crack was always good; politics were seldom discussed and sectarianism only raised its head openly as the twelfth of July drew near.

On St Patrick's night we had a great sing-song. One of the customers sang 'Kevin Barry' for my benefit while I was persuaded to render 'The Sash' in pidgin Irish, a sort of musical compromise.

There was always a recimatation or, as some would say, a recitation. The following, penned by Robert Calvert, was most popular.

In a mean abode on the Shankill Road lived a man named Billy Bloat
He had a wife, the curse of his life, who continually got his goat
So one day, at dawn, with her nightdress on, he cut her bloody throat.

With razor gash he settled her hash, oh, never was
  crime so quick
But the drip, drip, drip on tne pillowslip of her
  lifeblood made him sick
And the pool of gore on the bedroom floor grew
  clotted and cold and thick.

And yet he was glad he had done what he had when
  she lay there stiff and still
But a sudden awe of the angry law struck his heart
  with an icy chill
So to finish the fun so well begun he resolved
  himself to kill.

He took the sheet from his wife's coul' feet and
  twisted it into a rope
And he hanged himself from the pantry shelf, 'twas
  an easy end, let's hope
For in the face of death with his last dying breath he
  solemnly cursed the Pope.

But the strangest turn to the whole concern is only
  just beginning,
He went to Hell but his wife got well and she's still
  alive and sinning,
For the razorblade was German made but the sheet
  was Belfast linen.

As the bottles and half-uns flowed, one customer, above
the sound of 'When Irish Eyes are Smiling', whispered to me
with a friendly and knowing wink, 'Y'know, we're all Paddys
beneath the skin.' He took another meditative slug from his
Guinness and continued: 'If youse fenians would just catch
yourselves on and stay quiet, everything would be okay.'

We fenians, as far as I could figure out, weren't doing
anything to catch ourselves on about, but maybe your man
knew something I didn't know, so I said nothing. He and I used
to discuss politics or what passes for politics in Belfast. I was getting involved in housing agitation and used to argue that the
desperate housing conditions suffered by both the unionist and
anti-unionist working class showed the need for unity by us
against the common enemy. He used to say rather sheepishly

and just a wee bit shamefacedly when things became difficult, 'Awh well, let's not fall out over it. Whatever you say, say nothing.' Then, sadly, 'It'll be all the same in a thousand years.' Once, when a collection box was being waved rather provocatively under my nose, he encouraged me to make a donation and upset the collector by observing: 'G'wan, give a few bob, it's a worthy cause, the Orange widows, sure there couldn't be enough of them!'

On the night before the public holiday of 12 July I got the sack. Double time and a day off in lieu was the union rate for public holidays but my employer, a Catholic, refused to pay me the rate. He told me to finish up and collect my cards at the end of the week. 'Imagine asking for extra money, you ungrateful skitter; that's all the thanks I get for employing one of my own.' I kicked up a whole noration with the union branch secretary for months afterwards, but to no avail. Unemployed young people were a dime a dozen and the Knights of Columbanus had fused the Catholic business class and Catholic trade union officials into an old boy, ourselves alone institution.

Not that I was worried, it was more the principle of the thing. The customers were philosophical: 'That's the way,' they said, 'your own's always the worst.' 'You can't say I didn't warn you', one of them told me with a good-natured twinkle in his eye. 'As I'm always saying, you can't trust a fenian.' They lifted a collection for me and advised me to make up my lost wages from the till. I left after midnight and I think some of them were sorry to see me go. I was sorry to be going but delighted to be leaving my employer in the lurch on one of the busiest nights of the year as I walked out in the middle of a rush and strolled up the Shankill — the whole way past bonfires and public houses with their doors flung open. The place was swarming with people singing and dancing, acting the eejit, milling around, kicking the Pope.

> We are, we are, we are the Billy boys,
> We are, we are, we are the Billy boys,
> Up to our necks in fenian blood,
>
> . . . . .

Sunday-best suits and black bowler hats were the order of the day, or night as it was then. Point peelers were on duty, 'B' Specials chatted and drank with customers in pub doorways

and youngsters practised throwing their band major's maces
high in the air.

> As we march up and down
> On the road to Portadown
> Our drums we do batter
> Like the thunder
> And as the day grows near
> We'll fill the fenian hearts with fear
> On the twelfth of July in the morning.

At one street corner a man thrashed hell out of a
Lambeg drum, its terrorising staccato drawing yells of ap-
proval from the crowd while he, the blood flowing from his
wrists, seemed lost in some frenzied trance.

> Oh Dolly's Brae, oh Dolly's Brae, oh Dolly's Brae
>   no more
> For we'll kick the Pope and we'll kick him hard
> Right over Dolly's Brae.

On the Falls Road, as I approached it through the dark
side streets, all was quiet. A few people gathered at street corners talking and occasionally glancing towards the Shankill
from where the bonfire glow could be clearly seen and the
sounds of revelry clearly heard.

'They'll probably get a good day tomorrow', I heard
one man complain at the corner of Norfolk Street.

'They always do', replied his companion. 'Sure,
they've got God on their side. . . .'

That was 1966. The civil rights agitation had yet to
come. Norfolk Street, three years later, was reduced to ashes.
As your man would have said, 'Everything would have been
okay . . . if you fenians would just catch yourselves on.'

> In Dublin there's a man,
> And they say he has a plan
> He has 5,000 men or more they say,
> But we will get a rope
> And we'll hang your f . . . Pope,
> On the twelfth of July in the morning.

Perhaps if the British and loyalist ruling class had conceded the demands for one man one vote, one family one house and the abolition of the Special Powers Act, Norfolk Street and all those other burnt-out streets would still be standing today. But then, perhaps not. To have done so would have meant abolishing the Six County state; and that would never have done. And therein lies just one of the reasons why the fenians have yet to catch themselves on; and, despite the present carry-on, things, for the loyalists, will never be the same again. And that is good for us all, Catholics and Protestants alike. It'll never be the same again . . . even in a thousand years.

Cocker and Company

I am a wee falourie man, a rattling roving
    Irishman
I can do all that ever you can for I am a wee
    falourie man.

Belfast Street Song

LOCAL legend has it that some of the kidney pavers which covered the streets of the Falls Road were used to decorate the courtyards in Divis Flats — surely the only claim which that monstrosity has to architectural nicety. Today the flagstones which replaced them are vanishing also, victims of twelve years of street fighting, and pavements are so uneven now that one has to step carefully through the dark streets at night.

Now, what this has to do with Cocker and Company will come out in a minute. The system of macadamising road surfaces was named after its inventor John L. MacAdam. Another MacAdam, Robert S., was one of the owners of the Soho foundry in Townsend Street. He and I share the same family name, MacAdaimh. He was a collector of anecdotes and more importantly a man greatly interested in the Irish language. He brought to Belfast, for the purpose of translating Irish manuscripts, a number of Gaelic scribes including Hugh Mac-Donnell and Peter Galligan, who lived in the Millfield area. MacAdam also published over five hundred Ulster Gaelic proverbs and the very interesting narrative of the wars of 1641 by Friar O'Mellan, chaplain to Phelim O'Neill, which MacAdam had translated from the Irish. His efforts to preserve some record of our Gaelic heritage are well chronicled in Brendan Ó Buachalla's splendid book *I mBéal Feirste Cois Cuan.*

Belfast has always had its share of local characters and wits, and as far back as 1837 Robert MacAdam recorded in his notes stories of the railway stoker who described slow-burning anthracite coal as damned antichrist, of the bookseller who ordered as a medical work De Lome's *On the Constitution* and of bed warming pans being exported by accident by a Belfast merchant to the West Indies where they were sold at a great profit after being modified for use as skimmers for sugar pans.

In the 1820s street musicians included Cocky Bendy, a very small bow-legged man who knew the tune to play at every house he visited. 'Garryowen', 'Patrick's Day' and the 'Boyne Water' were his best paying airs.

Black Sam, another street character was a black man who had highly popular performing dogs and William Scott or Tantra Barbus was a notorious and eccentric street pedler and hawker. He was born in Ballynahinch in 1778 but never visited County Down after the '98 rebellion because of an accusation that he acted as a spy during that period. So famous was he that after his death in 1833, a small book was published, *The Life of William Scott alias Tantra Barbus with numerous anecdotes connected with that eccentric character together with an elegy written on his death by a Gentleman in Belfast, printed for the Hawkers 1833.*

Cathal O'Byrne records in *As I Roved Out* how earlier, at the turn of this century, Belfast street-singers Alex McNicholl and Arthur Quinn, who used to perform regularly in North Street, and other unnamed ballad makers interchanged homespun verses with 'The Rose of Tralee', 'The Bard of Armagh' and 'The Garden Where the Praties Grow'. He also recalls the woman ballad singer who would change the words and the mood of 'Dobbin's Flowery Vale' to suit her own mood, ending:

> An' to hell with you, an' Armagh too,
> An' Dobbin's flowery vale.

In the streets of the Falls at that time wandered Nicholas Ward, a blind singer who specialised in 'The Smashing of the Van', 'Clare's Dragoons', 'The West's Awake' and 'The Felons of Our Land'. Through these streets came the hurdy-gurdy man, and small groups of musicians, and tap dancers who carried their own dancing boards. People sat at their doors, all the better to enjoy such entertainment and whole streets joined in community singing and crack, often sitting up late into the night.

In more recent times I recall a street singer, cap in hand, knocking on doors and filling Abercorn Street with the air of many a patriotic tune. I was much surprised therefore, while cutting with my granny through the back streets of the Shankill Road, to spy the man putting on the same performance for the benefit of the residents there. My granny, suffice to say, wasn't at all taken aback and as we drew within earshot I realised why. Instead of 'Seán South of Garryowen' our enterprising balladeer was giving forth 'Abide with Me' and other religious offerings. I think he winked at me as we passed by and he certainly jingled his capful of coppers towards us in a decidedly cavalier fashion as he rendered his version of 'Nearer my God to Thee'.

Street singers, of course, weren't the only entertainers to tread our back streets. My Uncle Paddy recalls Oiney Boike, whose name lives on yet in local jargon. He used to sit the children along the kerb stone — the pavements were higher affairs in those days — where they swayed slowly from side to side while chanting 'Oiney Boike, Oiney Boike' as he conducted them and danced to their accompaniment. My Uncle Paddy reckons that Oiney Boike is a Belfast bastardisation of the Irish *Eoineen beag,* and he's probably right.

Another uncle of mine, Alfie, remembers a character of that period with illusions of grandeur known as the 'Duke of Millfield' who used, like an early John Cleese, to walk with great loping strides while holding a small soap container before him, for all the world like some noble personage bearing a valuable casket. Then there was John Donnelly of Cinnamond Street, alias Dr McNab, who sang with great fervour and a lisp 'St. Tewesa of de Woses' and 'Bootiful Dwema'. John, who hated his other nickname, 'Vinegar Bottle', was prone to attack those who dared to tease him and on more than one occasion actually threw his accordion at such tormentors. The queue at the old Ritz cinema on the Grosvenor Road was one of his more lucrative pitches, when he wasn't playing around the pubs, and he and Harry Tully, another street musician, used to do battle to get playing there.

Willie John McCorry recollects following Jimmy Madden for a blow on his tin whistle. Jimmy played on Friday nights, when the mill workers were paid, and Willie John's music lessons were always interrupted by Jimmy's impatient 'Hurry up, there's people coming'. An equally well known figure was blind Dan McAuley who was so tormented by local youngsters that he developed the painful habit of striking out at any passerby unlucky enough to come within the swing of his walking stick. He lived at the corner of Abyssinia Street, and he must have been equal only to Bunny Rice who boxed with shadows, and with any available pedestrian, on street corners throughout the Falls. Egged on by locals, Bunny was a daunting adversary as I found out to my embarrassment on more than one occasion at the corner of Sultan Street.

Big Joe Walsh, living yet, was in regular attendance at all Falls Road funerals. Weeping real tears and slobbering profusely into a large handkerchief, he accompanied most corpses from the area on their last journey to Milltown and was so much a local institution that attendance by anyone at a number of funerals was invariably described as being 'like Joe Walsh'. Afterwards Joe would retire to a local public house where he proceeded to get 'drunk' on a pint of lemonade. Joe, like all true Falls Road characters, was a 'harmless cretur', a source of innocent amusement who was well liked by people of the area.

Paddy-with-the-glass-eye, in my childhood days, used to beseech us while we taunted him to 'say a prayer for our mothers'. Once when mine was ill he told me he was praying for her. I held Paddy in some awe ever afterwards when my mother not only got better but produced a new baby into the bargain. In answer to the catechism question 'Who made the world?' Paddy, his glass eye peering blankly at the heavens, would reply: 'God made the world but me da carried the bricks for him.'

The area also boasted a number of strong men — mostly quiet hard-working individuals like Paul Jones from Scotch Street who was employed in the docks. Paul was well known for his unorthodox method of docking dog's tails. Most dog owners nowadays have their dog's tails cut by a vet or a doggie man but Paul Jones performed this task by simply biting off the offending item. He featured once in a weight-lifting contest in Diamond's pub in Millford Street — later in the 'sixties the venue, as Terry's Bar, for a revival of traditional music in Belfast. Paul was the only contestant to succeed in lifting a barrel of porter with two fingers from a bar room floor up to the bar counter.

John James Hagens was a quiet man who became fiercely hostile towards peelers when he had a few pints. Stripped to the waist, he fought off many an R.I.C. man and continued the practice when that force became the R.U.C. On one historic occasion the peelers suffered such a heavy defeat and John James was going at them with so much success that they only overwhelmed him when one peeler, Billy Pepper, thought of handcuffing him to a handcart. And that's the way that John James was taken, surrounded by battered peelers, to the barracks.

From Baker Street came Porky Flynn, another strong man, known to wheel a handcart with five or six hundredweight of scrap on it. Porky set off at four-thirty every morning to tour the city centre for scrap metal. He never owned a clock or watch but arose punctually with the aid of a candle which he had measured to go out at the time he wished to get up. Porky and his colleagues, rag men, refuse men and the like, could have exchanged their handcarts, at the cost of thirty shillings a week, for a horse and cart from Horsey Hughes at his yard in Servia Street. Horsey, well known also for his great strength, used after midnight on New Year's Eve, to lead or ride a horse into neighbours' houses. In more recent years another member of the family, Yako Hughes, continued this custom, using a donkey on occasions instead of a horse, until his death in tragic circumstances in 1980.

Before Yako's time Jimmy Duffin could be seen and heard making his way from Seán McKeown's public house in Lemon Street. Jimmy, a quiet enough chap while in the pub, commenced singing, his hand cupped *sean nós* style over his ear, as soon as he hit the street. Between songs he argued loudly with himself or shouted and guldered, oblivious of strangers' stares or the knowing smiles of local people. At times he would inform onlookers 'you're inconjudical' before continuing with his singing.

Paky and Maggie McCoo, a brother and sister, lived rough or in a flat above Kivlahan's bar in Cinnamon Street and were institutions around the locality. Maggie sometimes pushed an old pram and was accompanied occasionally by another chap. He was an Irish speaker and reputedly a competent organist from County Armagh, and Maggie and he often shared tuppence-worth of chips in Malachy Morgan's. Today people like Maggie and Paky would be called dipsos or winos. Perhaps they were so-called in those days also but if so it was only by those who didn't know them. The Falls Road people treated them as friends and Paky, who was in and out of prison for short periods on begging charges, was always looked after by the political prisoners. He and his colleagues lived similar life styles in the Loney area, surfacing after the night's sleep from beneath an old van or lorry to get breakfast in some friendly house.

One story told about Paky concerns his considerable gymnastic ability. One morning he got a bowl of cold black tea from Mrs McGinn at the corner of Curry Street. Paky topped the tea up with a touch of meths or wine and drained the bowl. Then, putting both his hands on the lamp post outside Mrs McGinn's, he pushed himself straight out until he was at right angles to the lamp post, three or four foot high and parallel to the ground. Then, with a wink to Mrs McGinn and a word of thanks for the tea, he proceeded on his way.

In more recent times another street character, a hawker who used to live rough, was Frank McCaul. Frank made a small fortune and got his nickname 'Fr Peyton' by selling photographs of the highly popular rosary crusade priest, Fr Peyton, as well as handkerchiefs and other knick-knacks. Frank's sales of handkerchiefs boomed during internment when they were much in demand by prisoners' relatives who despatched them to Long Kesh where the internees converted them into small hand-printed wall hangings.

Frank was to die in his sleep behind St Peter's Church in the black taxi in which he was sheltering for the night. Winter, as so often, took its toll.

Most of the street characters, hawkers and drop-outs frequented the many pubs along the Cullingtree Road fringe of the Loney. So relaxed, and illegal, were their Sunday drinking hours that this part of the area was known locally as Omeath. In the early 'seventies, with a temporary boom in shebeens, the same sense of dry humour echoed in the names of these drinking establishments. In Leeson Street we had 'The Cracked Cup', so called because it was situated in Eddie McGuigan's old shop from which Eddie used to sell delph to the ragmen. 'The Frying Pan' at the corner of Balaclava Street and Raglan Street got its name from the owner's eagerness to supply a bowl of stew or a fry at seven o'clock in the morning for those remaining on the premises. 'Doctor Hook's', a former dentist's surgery, had similar drinking hours, opening at six-thirty in the morning and a definite port-of-call for those seeking a cure. In McDonnell Street 'The Nail Bomb', so called for obvious reasons, did an equally heavy trade.

Shebeens to one side, the street characters of old have their contemporaries today: Fonsie Conway, Neddie Doherty, Starrs Kelly and all those unknowns who enrich life in every generation — like the anonymous scribe who was moved to write in large gable-size letters 'F...1690, WE WANT A REPLAY', or the woman who admonished a black British soldier with the words: 'To think I spent years giving the priest money for the black babies and now you have the cheek to come over here and torture the life out of us.' Or the lady who chided a British Army major for sending troops into a back entry after a group of youngsters. 'He hasn't enough sense to order his own dinner. Sending youse out to do his dirty work.' Then to the major: 'Come on out of that jeep and fight your own battles.' When he ignored her challenge telling her to 'F... off', she retorted, 'Yiz are all the same, yiz think you know everything. I cudn't like ye even if I rared yeh. Hell's gates and somebody blows yiz up. Then youse'll get some sense. Annoying people with your oul carry on. Lads can't even stand at their own corner. Someday the shoe'll be on the other fut, then ye'll know what side your bread's buttered on. Go away on home and leave us in peace. And take lappy lugs (the major) with youse. God help his poor wife. My heart goes out to her. At least with my Paddy if I've nothing to eat I've something to luk at. Imagine that poor woman waking up in the morning with your big watery gub in the bed beside her. Ya big long drink of water, giving your orders there. You think you're the fellah in the big picture. If I was a man I'd go through you like a dose of salts. You cudn't fight your way out of a wet paper bag.' And then, as the Brits left without their intended captives, she concluded, 'God forgive youse for making me make an exhibition of myself in the street. Them wee bucks showed youse the road home. There's better men in the Children's Hospital. You cudn't catch the cold.'

Another British Army foot patrol had a similar experience in Marquis Street when they chanced to stumble upon Neddy Doherty and Starrs Kelly. The senior Brit commenced to conduct an ID check on our two heroes and having established their names he proceeded to ascertain their addresses.

'Roight, moite', he addressed Neddy, 'what's your 'ome haddress?'

'I live everywhere and anywhere', replied Neddy.

'I must 'ave a proper haddress.'

'Well, put down the summer house in the Dunville Park.'

The Brit in exasperation scribbled furiously in his notebook and turned to Starrs who despite his fondness, along with Neddy, for an occasional snort of vino was always tidily dressed in yellow boots, Paddy hat and check suit.

'Where do you live?' asked the Brit.

'None of your business', answered Starrs with considerable dignity.

'I must have an address!' the Brit declared impatiently.

'What have you down for him?' queried Starrs. 'No fixed abode', replied the Brit. 'Well, put down the same for me,' said Starrs with a straight face, 'I live up his stairs.'

As we would say down our way, Starrs is as stupid as a fox. Such Belfast parlance, not restricted to any particular district or sect, had a famous son in Cocker Murray from Leeson Street. Our dog, Cocker, is so called in his memory and Falls Road republicans or ex-internees have loads of stories of Cocker's rather unique turns of speech. One describes a period when Cocker worked on the construction of Ballymurphy's Corpus Christi Church. (Joe Cahill, incidentally, was the foreman on that job and myself and two compatriots put up the railings. Never did get paid but that's another story.) Anyway Cocker had gathered, as was common practice, scrap pieces of wood for some household purpose. He returned to find that the nipper had used his blocks to kindle the fire to brew up the day's tea. In exasperation Cocker exclaimed, 'What the bloody hell do you think you're doing. You've burned up all my wood. Do you think the bloody stuff grows on trees?'

Another time, during a coal shortage, Cocker borrowed his brother-in-law's electric fire. In the bar that night his friends advised him against using such a device. 'You're mad,

Cocker,' they reasoned, 'that thing's dead expensive. It'll ate up your electricity.'

'Ach, I'm not worried about that', replied Cocker. 'It's not my fire. It's the brother-in-law's.'

Or, witnessing an incident in which a cat only narrowly escaped being knocked down by a passing motor vehicle, Cocker observed: 'Did youse see that? If that cat had been a dog it would have been a dead duck.' On one memorable occasion Cocker drew the attention of two local republican activists to a hovering helicopter: 'That's very fishy looking, you know. It's been stuck up there for twenty minutes in the same place. It must be broke down.'

Not that Cocker was stupid. Far from it. He was a kind man who delighted in making people laugh at life. Once in returning from Casement Park he meditated while passing Milltown Cemetery 'If God spares us, it won't be long 'til we're all in there.' And that seems a fitting note on which to end this brief look back on local characters and local crack. Long may their memory last.

Pawn Shops and Politics

Time has triumphed, the wind has scattered all,
Alexander, Caesar, empires, cities are lost
Tara and Troy flourished a while and fell
And even England itself, maybe, will bite the
dust.

Anon. Translated from the Irish by Brendan Kennelly

IN 1960 or thereabouts I transferred from St Finian's School,
via St Gabriel's to St Mary's in Barrack Street. On our way
home from school we walked along Divis Street and up the
Falls, spending our bus fares in one of the many shops which lit-
tered our route. On brisk autumn evenings, with leaves
carpeting the pavement and the road bustling with people, the
great linen and flax mills made a formidable backdrop while,
facing them, cheek to cheek, the rows of small shops served the
miscellaneous needs of local customers. There were a couple of
stretches of the road which I particularly favoured. From
Northumberland Street up as far as the Baths, along the convent wall by St Dominic's or alongside Riddell's field.

Paddy Lavery's pawn shop at Panton Street did a roaring trade in those days, its windows coming down with family
heirlooms, bric-á-brac, clocks, boots, even fishing rods, and in-

side, rows and rows of Sunday-morning-going-to-Mass-suits, pledged between Masses to feed the family or pay the rent. There was a horse trough at Alma Street and an old green Victorian lavatory facing it, beside the baths. In Dunville Park the fountain occasionally worked, cascading water around those who defied the wackey to paddle in the huge outer bowl.

In Divis Street a woman sold us hot home-made soda farls and pancakes plastered with jam. Brother Beausang packed us into the *Ard Scoil* for oral exams to win a place in the Donegal Gaeltacht; Ducky Mallon taught us our sevens; and lunch breaks were spent playing football beside the glass factory and afterwards seeing who could pee the highest in the school bog. Handball at gable walls in St Mary's, or cards and cigarettes for the big lads, were normal lunch time diversions.

We were all part of a new generation of working class Taigs, winning scholarships to grammer schools and 'getting chances' which, as our parents and grandparents frequently reminded us, they never had. We wore school uniforms — a fairly new and expensive luxury — and were slightly bemused to see our mirror reflections in Austin's, the school outfitters, just below Dover Street. I always noticed that the shop facing Austin's had its name sign painted in Irish. You could buy hurling sticks in another shop just below that, while almost opposite our school Wordie's kept their great shire horses in unique multi-storied stables.

Summer evenings were spent in the Falls Park playing hurling and football with infrequent formal handball sessions at the handball alley in St Malachy's. During the winter we cadged money for the Clonard, Broadway or Diamond picture-houses or for the baths and, exams to one side, life was pleasant and uneventful. Divis Flats weren't there then; instead a flour mill dominated the landscape. Victor's ice-cream parlour sold smokies, and Raffo's on the opposite side of the street offered scallops — one for a penny. Gerry Begley and Paddy Elliot, stalwarts of Dwyers Gaelic Athletic Club became my local heroes as they established themselves as experts on the hurling and football pitches of MacRory, Corrigan and the Falls parks.

Men walked greyhounds up the road or further afield and pigeon fanciers admired their birds tumbling, free from backyard sheds, into the early dusk, while the street pigeons or hokers quarrelled with sparrows and starlings over their evening meal. Jim McCourt from Leeson Street delighted us all by

winning an Olympic medal while John Caldwell, who hailed from Cyprus Street, boxed his way to a world championship title. We learned little of local or national history at school and had no sense of history as we passed through streets as historic as any in Ireland.

From the school at Barrack Street we passed by the Farset, which one teacher by name of 'Dirty Dick' Dynan told us could be seen from behind the houses in Durham Street. The houses are now gone, replaced by a car park, but the Farset can be seen still the same. We regularly dandered up Pound Street, knowing nothing of its history or even the old barracks which gives Barrack Street its name.

There were three R.U.C. barracks in our day: one at Hastings Street, one at Springfield Road and another at Roden Street, flanking the area on its three sides. A fourth, at Cull-

Lena's shop, now demolished.

intree Road, had only recently been replaced. Not that we were worried or even interested in such places. Nowadays, of course, with heavily fortified British Army and R.U.C. barracks and forts dotted strategically throughout West Belfast it is difficult to remain disinterested or neutral about their existence. It is especially so, in wet wintry times, when the Falls Road, washed grey by drizzling rain and suffering from the ravages of war and redevelopment, appears bleak and shabby, with the omnipresent foot patrols of British soldiers treading carefully through back streets a threatening intrusion into an area hostile to their presence.

Not that British soldiers are a new feature of the scenery in West Belfast. Since its days as a country lane raids and harassment have been occupational hazards suffered by residents of the Falls Road.

The Belfast *Newsletter* of 23 May 1797 records for example:

> At four o'clock in the evening Lieutenant
> General Lake directed Colonel Barber and Mr
> Fox (town mayor) to proceed with as much ex-
> pedition as possible to the cotton manufactory
> of Robert Armstrong on the Falls Road. Arriv-
> ing there before two persons, who were on the
> watch, could give an alarm, they caught a
> smith and his assistant forging pikes and, on
> threatening them with immediate death, they
> produced sixteen they had secreted in an adja-
> cent house, newly forged. A detachment from
> the Monaghan militia, and some yeomanry
> who followed, were so incensed at seeing those
> implements of destruction that they smashed
> the forge and levelled it to the ground. The
> pikes were then hung around the villains who
> were marched prisoners to the town.

A better known testimony of such raids is an expression which is often used even today by older Belfast people when unexpected visitors arrive: 'They're in on us and not a stone gathered.' It harks back to the days when cobblestones, locally known as kidney pavers or pickers, were used against British Army and R.I.C. raiding parties.

My first personal recollection of such raids was in 1964 when carefree and sleepy-headed I noticed on the way to school a tricolour displayed in a shop in Divis Street, just down from Percy Street opposite St Comgall's School. That evening a character, better known now than then, by name of Paisley threatened to march on Divis Street and remove the offending flag. Our curiosity, further aroused by a warning from our Christian Brother teachers to go straight home and not dilly-dally in Divis Street, led dozens of us to gather and peer into the window of what we were to discover was a Sinn Féin election office. Further encouragement was supplied by the R.U.C. who sledge-hammered their way into the premises and seized the flag. It was with some satisfaction, therefore, the following day that we witnessed a large crowd replacing it, an occasion for a most defiant rendering of *Amhrán na bhFian* and the subject of some schoolboy speculation upon what would happen next.

What happened next, of course, was the Divis Street riots, an exercise which we found most educational, though in truth it wasn't much of a spectator sport, with the R.U.C. being unable or unwilling to distinguish between curious scholars and full-blooded rioters. Some of us learned quickly that it was as well to be hanged for a stone as a stare and thus I found myself after homework had been cogged, folding election manifestos in the Felons Club, above Hector's shop in Linden Street. The republican candidate, Liam McMillan, lost his deposit — as did all the Sinn Féin candidates — but I suspect with hindsight that the electioneering was geared more to canvassing recruits than votes and in that it undoubtedly succeeded.

In the months afterwards children playing in the streets parodied the then current Perry Como song, 'Catch a Falling Star', to rhyme during hopscotch and skipping games:

> Catch a falling bomb and put it in your pocket,
> Never let it fade away.
> Catch a falling bomb and put it in your pocket,
> Keep it for the I.R.A.
> For a peeler may come and tap you on the shoulder
> Some starry night,
> And just in case he's getting any bolder
> You'll have a pocket full of gelignite.

For those old enough to recall Perry Como, it sounds better if you sing it. And if you're moved to go that far you might as well get a bit of rope and skip. That way you'll get the mood of the whole thing. Of course, youngsters are still parodying·popular songs and turning them into their own little songs of resistance. In back streets and school yards throughout the Six Counties you'll hear rhymes which instruct British soldiers on how to dispose of their plastic bullets, and popular I.R.A. actions are committed to verse with a speed which amazes many adults.

In the build-up and aftermath of the Divis Street riots there was some awakening of national consciousness and a few of us began to query, with candid curiosity, the state of the nation. We were puzzled by our description in official forms as British subjects and wondered as we passed the customs posts on our way to Bun Beag for a summer in the Gaeltacht what ex-

actly the border was. We were beginning to get a sense of our
essential Irishness, and events on the Falls Road served to whet
our political appetites. Before the 'sixties were over we would
be canvassing the streets of the Loney for support for our efforts
in opposing the building of Divis Flats. 'Low rents not high
flats' would be the cry as we picketed the corporation and all
others directly or indirectly involved; for this we would be
publicly chastised by the parish priest of St Peter's. From that
agitation would arise the West Belfast Housing Action Committee under whose auspices we squatted families from condemned houses, particularly in Mary Street, in newly built
flats. We would receive many summonses from the R.U.C.
and occupy many city centre offices in the process escaping im-
prisonment only because of the 'Paisley Amnesty'. So, too,
would emerge temporarily the West Belfast Unemployment
Action Committee, and by that time we were in the Civil Rights
Assocation and later the Central Citizens' Defence Committee
and all that grew from it, from barricades to today. But that was
all in front of us.

By the end of 1964 I was merely an interested part of a
small group which gathered in a dingy room in a Cyprus Street
G.A.A. Club to learn about Fenians and Fenianism,
colonialism, neo-colonialism, partition and British im-
perialism. Sinn Féin, then an illegal organisation, was beginning to expand once again and I was happy to be part of this new
expansion. The Special Powers Act, the ban on Sinn Féin and
on the *United Irishman* newspaper, the lack of adult suffrage,
discrimination in jobs and housing, the gerrymandering of
local government boundaries and the sectarian divisions which
were built into the Stormont structures all became real and
deeply felt grievances.

'Do you know', I remarked to Jamesie Magee as we
stood at the corner of Leeson Street and Getty Street, 'that you
can be imprisoned for singing a rebel song?'

'Sure, everybody knows that,' he replied with indif-
ference, 'sure, me da got six months once for burning a Union
Jack.'

'I didn't know that.'

'Ah, you see,' he retorted, 'you don't know everything,
do you?'

'I never said I did, did I?' Mortified at his suggestion, I
glared down towards the Varna Gap.

'Well, if I ever get time it'll be for more than burning a Union Jack', he continued. 'Josie had the right idea: he's in Canada. If I don't get a job soon I'm going to Australia. There's nothing in this place for anyone. If you had to pay for a living we'd all be dead.'

'Ach, it's not as bad as that', I asserted. 'A few changes here and there and we'd all be happy.'

'It's okay for you, still at St Mary's learning to be whatever you're learning to be. I've left school six months now and still no sign of work. If your ma or your granny weren't keeping you, you'd soon know your master. You jack in school and you'll see the difference.'

'You're putting the scud on me, Josie. C'mon and we'll go for a wee dander. Did you know that you can be whipped with a cat-o'-nine-tails under the Special Powers Act?'

'And you want me to stay here? Your head's a marley. If me da can raise the money I'm taking myself off out of it.'

And so he did. And shortly afterwards I jacked in school, and from then on *mar a deirtear, is é sin scéal eile* (as they say, that's another story). In the meantime, by some unnoticed, the Loney, Leeson Street and all that they meant have been erased and, the likes of it as Tomás Ó Criomtháin wrote in *An t'Oileánach*, will never be seen again.

Postscript

FR Dominic Crilly S.D.S., an old boy of St Peter's parish, gazed down from the newly erected Divis Tower as the redevelopment of the Falls area got under way and penned the following lines called 'Litany of the Streets'.

> The body of the parish lies stretched below the
>   Tower,
> Its main arteries are weakened and dying by the
>   hour,
> There are clots of bricks and mortar in the little
>   veins of the streets,
> And the talk is all of 'flitting' with everyone one
>   meets.
> But do you know the people who have lived here all
>   their lives,

Who have reared vast hosts of children in these tiny
    little hives?
Whose entries are their country lanes, whose lamp
    posts are the trees,
And the ridge tiles of the houses are the hills that
    bring the breeze.
Just enter any house there, morning, noon or
    night,
You will find the brasses gleaming and glowing fire
    alight,
They may be on the bureau or have lately lost their
    job,
But you'll get your cup of tea from the teapot on the
    hob.
The milkman, the 'assiety' man, the man who
    brings the bread,
Know the woes of every family, sick, missing,
    dying, dead,
But they also share the pleasure when joy has paid a
    call,
And they never need to knock the door, they come
    right to the hall!
But the pattern's quickly changing and the names
    will soon be gone,
And the homely kitchen houses will soon be quite
    forlorn,
When the new flats are all ready and the Housing
    Trust man calls,
To give new hope to many but the 'black cap' to the
    Falls.
So from Albert Street and Alma Street, and
    Abercorn Street North,
Ardmoulin and Abyssinia Street, the people must
    go forth,
From historical Alexander Street, already well gone
    west,
Will go Baker Street and Boomer Street and Bow
    Street and the rest,
Bosnia Street and Bread Street, Brook Street and
    Belgrade,
Will be with Boundary Street and Balkan Street in
    Balaclava laid,

Cape Street, Cyprus Street, Cupar Street and
    Crane,
Will with Christian Place and Cullingtree fade into
    a lane.
Conway Street and Cairns Street further up the
    Falls,
With Dover, Divis, David and Derby lose their
    walls,
Then Dysart Street and Dunville, Dunlewey,
    Devonshire
Will share the fate of Durham and fade into the
    mire.
English Street and Elizabeth and Frere Street must
    go,
With Granville Street and Garnett Street the pace
    will not be slow,
The fate of poor old Gilford Street we all already
    know,
But Grosvenor Road and Grosvenor Place will have
    a later show.
Gibson Street and Getty Street with Irwin Street
    will fall,
And Inkerman with Leeson Street will soon receive
    the call.
Lincoln Street, Lemon Street, Lady, Lower
    Clonard,
With Mary and Merrion will go the way of
    Milford.
McDonnell and McMillan will go with
    Marchioness,
With Milliken and Milan that will be some
    hundreds less,
Nail Street, Norfolk Street, Northumberland,
    North Howard,
And Osmond, Odessa and Ormonde will be
    ploughed.
Knocking down Pound Street made the senses reel,
And this will happen also to Plevna Street and Peel,
While Panton Street and Percy Street will fall with
    Quadrant,
And Ross and Raglan Street will be reduced to
    sand.

Roumania Street and Ross Place and Sevastopol
　　will cease,
And Scotch Street and Sultan Street with Spinner
　　see decease,
Sorella Street and Servia Street with Theodore and
　　Ton,
Will disappear with Varna now the work is nearly
　　done.
Already Whitehall Court has disappeared from
　　view,
There may be some I haven't mentioned, streets
　　and people just as true,
But I'm sure that in the future whatever ill befalls,
The glory of St Peter's will still shine around the
　　Falls.

Notes

Page

1 *I dandered along* I strolled along
2 *a visit to the 'broo'* to the Bureau — the Labour Exchange
Kansas Glen corruption of McCance's Glen, below Colin Glen
3 *peelers* policemen
R.U.C. Royal Ulster Constabulary
4 *being chased by 'the wackey'* the watchman
playing marleys marbles
a doffer a linen-worker
her rubber rubber apron
picker an instrument used for picking or cutting the ends of the linen threads.
16 *An Cumann Beag and the 'Old Felons'* The buildings of the old industrial school were used by the 'Felons' Club', a social club for Republicans who had been interned or jailed for political activities. Some years ago they moved to new premises, hence the 'Old Felons'.
18 *the Volunteers, Presbyterians all* a part-time force set up initially to protect the Anglo-Irish colony in Ireland against a possible French invasion during the American War of Independence, 1776-83. They then played a leading role in the agitation, led by Henry Grattan, for legislative independence for the Irish colonial parliament, 1782. Though entirely Protestant, they also urged an end to the Penal Laws against Catholics. They declined after 1783 but in Belfast some of them eventually joined the United Irishmen.
24 *Omeath* a village in County Louth, on Carlingford Lough, which was still Irish-speaking until the beginning of this century.
30 *a rapper-upper* was paid to wake the mill-workers in time for them to get to work, often by rapping on the upstairs windows of the houses with a long pole.
31 *the R.I.C.* Royal Irish Constabulary; the name for the police force in the thirty-two counties of Ireland up to 1922 when police in the twenty-six counties were reconstituted as the *Gárda Síochána* and the police in the six counties were re-named the Royal Ulster Constabulary.
the mad month of July in the weeks before and after the main Orange (Protestant/Unionist) celebration on 12 July each year there was a series of smaller Orange parades and ceremonies and Orange fervour reached its highest pitch. Orangemen often ceased to talk to Catholic neighbours or workmates, with whom they were otherwise friendly, during July.

33 *the Union* the workhouse

52 *The Irish Volunteers* were formed in 1913 to oppose the Ulster Volunteers (U.V.F.) who were threatening to resist Home Rule in the North. They split in 1914 when John Redmond and the Irish Home Rule party urged them to join the British army in the First World War. The minority who opposed Redmond were led by P. H. Pearse and took part in the 1916 Rising. After 1916 they were commonly called Sinn Féin Volunteers until the autumn of 1919 when they officially came under the authority of Dáil Éireann and were known as the Irish Republican Army.

66 *the Specials* the Ulster Special Constabulary set up in November 1920 by the British government. It was the main arm of the Northern government until the R.U.C. was established in mid-1922. The Specials included a full-time section, the 'A' force and two part-time sections, the 'B' and 'C' forces. The 'A' and 'C' Specials were disbanded at the end of 1925. The 'B' Specials were retained until 1970.

66 *cage-car* open military lorry with a wire cage to ward off grenades.

79 *slagging and reddeners* teasing and blushing faces

81 *fornenst* next to

91 *knollered* caught
blimping looking

92 *you're dead fly* you're very cunning
spondooliks money
champ potatoes mashed with scallions and butter

93 *gurning* complaining
mixed-ups assorted sweets

94 *cog my ecker* copy my homework
sleekit cunning, sly

95 *scoutsie* lift
dolls women
gravy-ring doughnut

96 *poke* twisted paper cone

97 *odds* small change

98 *the Sprinky* the Springfield Road

99 *guldered* shouted
clodding throwing

100 *lurchers* cross-bred greyhounds

103 *a quare gunk* a shock

108 *Prods and Micks* Protestants and Catholics

109 *sally rod* Prod
Dominic Savio a boy martyr
a sprassy a sixpenny piece

115 *fenians* a generic term used to describe Catholics; the name comes from the Fenian movement, the Irish Republican Brotherhood, a secret society founded in 1858 to fight for Irish independence.

116 *noration* row

119 *I am a wee falourie man* the origin of 'falourie' is obscure. David Hammond suggests it may mean 'forlorn' or be a variant of 'Gable'oury man' in English ballads meaning Gabriel, holy man.

124 *So relaxed, and illegal, were their Sunday drinking hours that this part of the area was known locally as Omeath.* Omeath, being just over the border, was one of the nearest spots where Northerners could avail of the South's more liberal licensing laws especially Sunday opening. Omeath's pubs reputedly never closed.

129 *taught us our sevens* Irish dancing

130 *working-class Taigs* working-class Catholics

134 *the 'Paisley Amnesty'.* In May 1968 after the ousting of Captain Terence O'Neill, the Northern Prime Minister, his successor, Major Chichester-Clark announced an amnesty for public order offences. Its primary purpose was to release the Rev. Ian Paisley who was serving a jail sentence for obstructing a civil rights march. As a spin-off charges were also dropped against a number of civil rights activists.

137 *on the bureau* on the dole

the 'assiety' man the insurance man.

Note on street names

A number of the streets in the Lower Falls area have names connected with the Crimean War and the Balkans e.g. Raglan Street, Balaclava Street, Sevastopol Street, Inkerman Street, Odessa Street, Alma Street, Plevna Street, Sultan Street, Balkan Street, Cyprus Street, Varna Street, Servia Street, Bosnia Street, Belgrade Street, Roumania Street. These streets were built by the Ross family, owners of a local linen mill, who had prospered as a result of the Crimean War. They used their profits to expand their mill and to build houses for their workers and to rent.

Another small group of streets off the Springfield Road have even more exotic names like Kashmir Road, Bombay Street, Cawnpore Street, Lucknow Street and Benares Street, commemorating the Indian Mutiny and the heyday of the British Empire in India in the later nineteenth century when they were built.

At first glance another street in the Beechmount area looks as if it too belongs to this 'Indian' group — Amcomri Street. In fact it commemorates the widespread evictions of Catholic families in Belfast in the 1920s. Amcomri Street was built with contributions from the United States to re-house evicted families and its name is short for American Committee for Relief in Ireland.

Select Bibliography

George Benn, *A History of the Town of Belfast,* Davidson Books, Bally-nahinch, County Down, 1979 (facsimile of 1823 edition).

R. M. Young, *Historical Notes of Old Belfast and its Vicinity,* Marcus Ward Press, Belfast, 1896.

H. A. McCartan, *The Glamour of Belfast,* Talbot Press, Dublin 1921.

F. J. Bigger, *Prehistoric and Historic Forts and Raths in the City and Vicinity of Belfast,* Belfast Naturalists' Field Club, 1894.

Cathal O'Byrne, *As I Roved Out,* S.R. Publishers, Wakefield, 1970.

George MacCartney, *Souveraigne of the Borough of Belfast,* 1707.

J. C. Beckett and R. E. Glasscock, (editors), *Belfast: Origin and Growth of an Industrial City,* BBC, London 1967.

Nora Connolly O'Brien, *Portrait of a Rebel Father,* Four Masters Press, Dublin, 1975.

Carmel Gallagher, *All Around the Loney-O,* published by the author, Belfast, 1978.

R. M. Fox, *James Connolly, the Forerunner,* The Kerryman, Tralee, 1946.

Proinsias Mac an Bheatha, *Tart na Córa: Saol agus Saothar Shéamais Uí Conghaile,* Foilseacháin Náisiúnta, Baile Átha Cliath, 1965.

Breandán Ó Buachalla, *I mBéal Feirste Cois Cuan,* An Clóchomhar, Baile Átha Cliath, 1968.

Andrew Boyd, *Holy War in Belfast,* Anvil Books, Tralee, 1969.

Andrew Boyd, *The Rise of the Irish Trade Unions 1729-1970,* Anvil Books, Tralee, 1972.

James Connolly, *The Reconquest of Ireland,* New Books, Dublin 1973.

J. O'Laverty, *An Historical Account of the Diocese of Down and Connor, Vol. I,* Davidson Books, Ballynahinch, County Down, 1980, (facsimile of 1878 edition).

Paddy Devlin, *Yes, We Have No Bananas,* Blackstaff Press, Belfast, 1981.

Pamphlets

Joe Graham, *Where the Lagan Flows.*

Jimmy Steele, *Patriot Graves.*

Saint John the Evangelist

Clonard Church and Monastery

Periodicals

The Irish News, The Belfast Newsletter, The Capuchin Annual, An Phoblacht/Republican News, The Irish Times, The Times (London).

The street songs and verses in the text are taken mostly from memory or primary sources. In many cases, because of space restrictions, I used only excerpts. For the more inquisitive reader, or singer, I would recommend David Hammonds' *Songs of Belfast,* Gilbert Dalton, Dublin, 1978, not least because he includes a musical score for each piece in his collection including some of those quoted here.

I would like to praise the sterling work done by the late Hugh Quinn in composing and collecting Belfast street songs. Unfortunately, I was unable to obtain any of his manuscripts though I came upon ample evidence of his diligence and handiwork.

Finally, thanks to the staff of the National Library for assistance with material on Bulmer Hobson, Seán MacDermott, Denis McCullough, on Belfast's educational system and on Danish settlements in Ireland.

THE MAN WHO MADE IRELAND: THE LIFE AND DEATH OF MICHAEL COLLINS
Tim Pat Coogan

"Superb...this will be a hard Life to beat." *Times Literary Supplement*

"Thanks to *The Man Who Made Ireland* readers here can get the full story of this good-humored patriot...[a] heroic account." *The New York Times Book Review*
$24.95 hardcover, $14.95 paperback

All orders must be prepaid (check, VISA, or Mastercard) and include $3.00 for postage and handling. To receive further information or to be put on our mailing list, please write, fax, or telephone the toll-free number below.

Roberts Rinehart Publishers
Post Office Box 666
Niwot, Colorado 80544

1-800-352-1985
1-303-652-3923 (FAX)